D0627887

THE WRITER'S GUIDE
TO TRAINING
YOUR DRAGON

Using Speech Recognition Software
to Dictate Your Book
and Supercharge
Your Writing Workflow

SCOTT BAKER

Access FREE private video training, exclusive to anyone who has bought this book. It's my personal way of saying thank you for your purchase.

To access the free training, go to:
http://eepurl.com/bQ4Y9X

When you enter your email address, you will be sent a private link to the video training. Don't worry – your email address will only be used to send you further videos and details of related releases, including free updates to this book. It will never, ever be shared with or sold to third parties, used for spam or any other purpose.

There is also a link to additional **FREE** resources at the very end of this book – everything from software and apps to microphones and voice recorders, all covered in detail throughout the following chapters. Don't miss it!

*For N, E and W, who no longer look at me
strangely when I'm talking to myself out loud.*

Contents

A Note from the Author - 13

Changes to this Edition - 13
PC Users - 14
Mac Users - 15
Dragon Anywhere - 16
Should You Update? - 16

Introduction - 19

What Is Different About This Book? - 23

Part One: First Things First - The Software - 26

Dragon Really Is The Only Option - 26
Mac vs PC - 27
Mobile Dictation - 30

Part Two: Hardware - The Right Tools for the Job - 35

Microphones: Garbage In = Garbage Out - 36
What about Wireless? - 43
Choosing Your Computer - 46
On the Go: Tablet Setups - 51

Microphone Setup - 55

Adjusting your levels - 57

Initial Voice Calibration in Dragon - 60

Training Texts - 65

Part Three: Software – Training your Dragon - 68

Word vs Text Editors: Think First Draft - 69

Your First Hurdle: Getting Used to Dictation - 72

Speed vs Accuracy and Obsessively Saving Your Profile - 76

Training Your Brain, Revisited - 79

Custom Words and Phrases - 83

Part Four: Next-Level Dictation - 89

Consistent Accuracy Anywhere, Anytime - 89

A Mic for Every Occasion - 91

Transcription: the Holy Grail of Dictation - 96

Part Five: Off and Running - 109

Invest in Both Software and Hardware - 109

Consider Your Workflow - 110

Perfection Is the Enemy of Progress - 112

Don't Train the Software to Learn Things You Didn't Write - 113

Write in Bursts and Embrace Transcription - 116
Using Dictation to Make Editing Easier - 117
What About Punctuation? - 121
Mac Users and the Roaming Cursor - 123

Afterword: Mission Accomplished - 126

Additional Resources - 130

A Note from the Author

An update on the latest versions of Dragon: v15 for PC and v6 for Mac

Changes to this Edition

Thank you for buying this book!

You are probably reading this because, like myself, you desperately want to increase your word count using dictation software. This updated edition of the book has been completely updated to include information on the various versions of Dragon available for both Mac and PC as of October 2016.

Here's the important thing to note: in terms of the techniques and equipment required to achieve consistently high dictation accuracy, *nothing has changed*. The recent updates to Dragon are, for the most part, incremental. Nuance has added what they call "Deep Learning" to the most recent versions of the product that claim to bring better long-term accuracy but regard this with a pinch of salt. With the right setup and techniques, your accuracy should consistently be extremely high anyway.

So, before you dive in to the book, here's what you need to know if you are about to buy a copy of Dragon or are thinking of upgrading.

PC Users

The current "consumer" versions of the product are Dragon NaturallySpeaking Home v13 and Dragon NaturallySpeaking Premium v13. Due to the restrictions (such as lack of transcription) in the Home version, I don't recommend it – get Premium instead.

The latest "professional" version (which is Premium with additional Enterprise-based features) is Dragon Professional Individual v15. This replaced Professional Individual v14 which simply used the same speech engine as Premium v13 but adds the new "Deep Learning" engine and Dragon Anywhere support. Confused yet?

Here's the simple version – **Dragon NaturallySpeaking Premium v13 and Dragon Professional Individual v15 are the current versions of the Windows software**. There are also specialist Legal and Medical versions but you can safely ignore these. So which should you buy? Dragon Premium is fine but if you want the new "Deep Learning" engine and Dragon Anywhere compatibility, get Professional Individual v15.

Mac Users

Nuance seems to have a real problem deciding what to call their product for the Mac. What started life as MacSpeech Dictate and Scribe became Dragon Dictate (up to v4), then Dragon for Mac 5 and is now **Dragon Professional Individual for Mac 6**. Make your mind up, Nuance!

Unlike the PC software which has separate Home, Premium and Professional versions, there is only one edition of Dragon for the Mac. The aforementioned v5 is, incredibly, the most stable version of the software (a dubious accolade as they are all pretty buggy) at the time of writing when updated to v5.0.5. It uses the same speech engine as Dragon Premium v13 and Professional v14 for Windows.

Dragon Professional Individual for Mac 6, released in September 2016, brings the new "Deep Learning" engine and Dragon Anywhere synchronisation to Mac users. It's also horrifically buggy. Hopefully Nuance will address this *very* quickly with updates – the software in its current form (already patched to little effect to v6.0.1 as of writing) feels like a rushed beta. It crashes frequently, is likely to result in lost work and can even bring your whole Mac to a halt. As it currently stands, I would exercise extreme caution with it.

If you are currently using a version of Mac OS

X (now renamed macOS) earlier than 10.11, be warned that Dragon 6 is not supported. The new software is only compatible with El Capitan or the newly-released Sierra.

Alternatively, regardless of your OS, keep using v5.0.5 for now or run the vastly superior PC version on your Mac – I'll tell you how later in this book.

Dragon Anywhere

This is the mobile version of Dragon for iOS and Android. It is a subscription product, costing $15 per month. While useful, it has significantly less features than the desktop versions of Dragon and requires a constant Internet connection to work.

You can sync your custom words with the new PC and Mac software, but that's it. For a better mobile solution, I recommend transcription – you can learn all about this in **Part Four** of this book.

Should You Update?

This brief note should bring you bang up-to-date with the various versions of Dragon and whether you should upgrade your current software. If you are buying for the first time, it makes sense to purchase the latest versions if only for the latest speech engines and longest technical support. To recap, these are Professional Individual v15 for Windows and v6 for the Mac – but bear in mind the latter, in particular, is already in need of a stability update. If you already own, say, Premium v13 or Dragon for Mac 5 then this book will significantly increase your accuracy and I'm not sure an upgrade is desperately needed at this stage.

Just for clarity, I will often simply refer to Dragon for the PC as "NaturallySpeaking" throughout this book. To distinguish between platforms, I'll use "Dragon for Mac" even though both now share the name "Dragon Professional Individual". Also, please note that the operating system previously known as Mac OS X will be referred to by its new title as of the Sierra release, macOS.

The information throughout this book has been updated to reflect the latest versions and, where necessary, I have added new content to each section to reflect any changes in the most recent software.

Okay, enough of this preamble. Get dictating!

Scott Baker
October 2016

Introduction

The pain was unbearable, like nothing I had ever experienced before.

I always thought a repetitive strain injury would be my downfall as a writer. I'd been warned about the dangers of carpal tunnel syndrome and other RSI-related ailments for years by colleagues who had suffered similar fates. I'd heard terrible, nightmarish scenarios of people who couldn't type for months at a time, who couldn't even turn a door handle or hold a cup. I'd used ergonomic keyboards and mice, even experimented with things like trackballs (not for me - but I really did try, honest) and thought I had done enough to safeguard myself.

I was sadly mistaken.

It wasn't the typing that took me out; it was the posture. Sitting, hunched over a keyboard for hours and hours each day, had finally caught up with me. It had started as a strange pinching sensation in my lower back, then a dull ache that refused to go away. Then, one morning, I simply couldn't stand up. Panic set in. The pain was like nothing on earth, enough to bring tears to anyone's eyes and debilitating to the point of sheer helplessness. I knew immediately what had happened. I had a herniated disc, or maybe several. I would be lying on my back for weeks, maybe even months.

My first thought was: *how the hell am I going to*

write? How am I going to make a living?

Like I said, I'd been warned. Most of the people I knew had experienced some form of RSI during their writing career; after all, pounding at a keyboard for long periods isn't exactly healthy. It's a bit like running – there's a relentless pressure on your joints when your feet slam against solid tarmac over and over. Typing is like a microcosm of that; tiny joints slamming against a smaller surface area, but with equally shallow depth. Keyboards have been getting thinner and thinner for years and, for many people, a laptop "chiclet" keyboard or even a tablet screen has become their writing implement of choice. That has resulted in even less resistance, even more chance to cause the tiny bones and nerves in your hands some serious damage.

But, as I found out when I faced up to the prospect of an undisclosed amount of time recuperating, it didn't really matter how I had been put out of action. The simple fact was this - I couldn't write. I wouldn't be able to sit upright for any length of time, so typing was well and truly out of the question. I was in no better a position than someone who had broken their wrists or had both hands set in plaster; I was equally as impotent, facing an unsure income for the next several months.

That was my biggest concern. How would I support my family? Like most authors, I hadn't reached the point of having a runaway, breakout hit; I earned my entire income from writing but was dependent on a reasonable level of production each month to keep fiction royalties flowing from the likes of Amazon, Kobo and iTunes. For many years prior to becoming a full-time fiction author, I'd been writing as a freelancer for magazines in the UK and had fortunately picked up a skill that could well turn out to be my saving grace.

Dictation.

If there's one thing that spurs you into working more than anything else, it's having a deadline. I've never been a fast typist; I can't "touch type" as we call it in the UK. I'm not quite a two finger hunt and pecker, either, but I can type with no more than three fingers at a time and have to look at the keyboard. That means my word count per minute is pretty low – around 45 WPM, probably better than average but certainly not stellar.

The problem with being 42 years old and unable to type quickly was twofold; firstly, I would have to learn keyboarding skills in order to improve and, two, as anyone with multiple children will know, there's barely enough time to get dressed and brush your teeth each day in addition to everything else. Shaving on a regular basis is a *real* luxury. Spending weeks or even months learning to touch type was out of the question for me. Luckily, there was another solution.

I had first started using Dragon dictation software back in the 1990s. I'd been working in the area of technology support for businesses at the time, and the software was both revolutionary and awful. It was a strange curiosity – expensive, the stuff of science fiction. I couldn't help but be intrigued by it, but the reality was that it didn't live up to the hype. Recognition was extremely poor, certainly not good enough to rely on to make a living. Some of the mistakes it made were downright laughable and, like many others at the time who tried it, it was consigned to a desk drawer, never to be touched again.

Fast forward 20 or so years, though, and things have changed dramatically. Luckily for me, I'd started using Dragon again before my debilitating back injury. It was those crazy deadlines, you see. How does someone who writes 40 words per minute put together a 4000 word article with 24 hours notice? With great difficulty, let me tell you. I got really tired really fast of staying up until two in the morning to finish pieces for my editor – that's where Dragon came in. I'd heard it had got better than all those years ago and, as it turned out, the rumours were true.

Now, lying on my back in a pit of despair, Dragon became my saviour. It can be yours, too. If repetitive strain injuries and slow typing speeds are a writer's Kryptonite, then Dragon is our nuclear weapon.

What Is Different About This Book?

Whether your intention is to prevent injury, safeguard your income during times when you are unable to write, or simply dramatically increase your word count, dictation software is one of the single most powerful tools in a writer's arsenal. Used correctly and set up with the right equipment, you could find yourself able to achieve startlingly high levels of accuracy, no matter where or when you write.

There are many excellent guides already out there on why you should use dictation software, the benefits of it and ways of adjusting your workflow to fit it into your writing life. Monica Leonelle, Chris Fox and Cindy Griggs all have superb books you can read covering everything from techniques that improve your dictation to drills to become more comfortable with it in practice.

The aim of this book, however, is simple – to get you as accurate as possible using Dragon *from day one*. I believe that poor accuracy is the number one reason most people give up on dictation software and never go back to it. That's a crying shame, as Dragon is now so accurate out-of-the-box with even the most unusual of accents that you should be able to start dictating effectively within your first hour of installing the software.

I have spent several years investigating the technical adjustments you can make to ensure your accuracy is extremely high from the very first day you use it. Some of this comes from use and some of it comes from tips and techniques passed on to me from experts within the industry. By combining this knowledge and presenting it to you in this book, one thing is certain – with the right set up and a small investment of time, you will be dictating at around 99% accuracy in most cases in almost no time. That doesn't mean Dragon won't make mistakes. You can, however, learn to not only anticipate those mistakes but work within them by employing little techniques (I call them "Insider Tips" that you will find of the end of each chapter) to make your first draft as clean and ready for revision as possible.

Don't be under any illusions. Setting up the software takes a small investment of time and you will need to be prepared for a financial outlay in order to consistently maintain good results without frustration. That doesn't mean you need to spend a lot of money – far from it – but you do need to be able to spend your money wisely. Don't waste your time or cash on substandard microphones and computers that provide an agonisingly slow dictation experience. This book will help you to set up your equipment correctly and train your Dragon efficiently to achieve outstanding results from day one that will only get better over time.

If you are new to dictation software, it is highly recommended that you read this book in a linear fashion. Although there are sections you may want to skip forward to, I have included vital information on hardware and setup of the software that even experienced users may not know about. There are many hidden tricks and techniques to get Dragon to work to its full potential – information I have gleaned from usage and talking to voice recognition professionals within the industry over many years.

I have to include the standard disclaimer that your mileage may vary, but if you commit to Dragon and follow the steps in this book, I can say with a high level of confidence that your writing workflow will be transformed. I have reached a point where my accuracy and output is so high that using the keyboard for anything other than editing is simply inefficient these days. With the help of this book, you can unleash the potential of this incredibly powerful tool and truly write at the speed of speech.

Part One: First Things First - The Software

Dragon Really Is The Only Option

Once you have made the decision to incorporate dictation into your workflow, the choice of software is simple. Right?

Well, not quite. Let me get this out of the way: if you are serious about doing this in any capacity, you must – repeat, *must* – use Dragon software from Nuance. Both Windows and macOS include built in voice recognition software, but it is limited in its usefulness. It's hard to argue with the price – they are both technically free, after all – and are a good way to try out dictation to see if it's for you. But be warned: you are likely to be disappointed with the results and it could put you off using dictation software completely.

Even Google Docs now has its own built-in dictation tool but, like the offerings from Apple and Microsoft above, it is not a good long-term solution. All share a common flaw in that they are unable to adapt to your voice, your speech patterns and vocabulary. Only Dragon can learn your writing style and adjust its algorithms (the clever mathematics the program is performing to turn your words into text on the screen) to improve over time. In fact, you'll find that if you take the time to correct Dragon's mistakes your accuracy will skyrocket. Dragon is one of the few programs that actually improves the more you use it as it constantly learns how you say certain words and adjusts the accuracy as a result.

By all means, try the free solutions out. For sending the odd letter or email they may well prove more than adequate, but for anything more serious (especially if your income depends on it) you simply have to invest in Dragon.

Mac vs PC

Even then, things aren't clear-cut. Do you have a Mac or a PC? The good news, at least on the surface of things, is that Nuance makes a version of Dragon for both platforms. The reality, though, is that the two programs – Dragon NaturallySpeaking for the PC and Dragon for Mac – are very different animals. It should be noted at this stage that both programs now go under the moniker of "Dragon Professional Individual" but, despite the name change, the PC version is still very much NaturallySpeaking in different clothing. The interface remains virtually unchanged since several versions ago and benefits greatly from many years as a stable and popular program.

Dragon NaturallySpeaking has been on the Windows platform for decades and, as a result, is a very mature program that performs superbly. The Mac version, however, wasn't originally Dragon software at all. It was originally called MacSpeech Dictate, had pretty patchy accuracy but, by virtue of being the only solution available, became the go-to software for Apple users.

Nuance bought MacSpeech Dictate and rebranded it with the Dragon name. As a result, the interface is very different to NaturallySpeaking and, until recently, was missing large sections of core functionality that Windows users enjoyed. The speech recognition engine used in both platforms is exactly the same, so recognition accuracy should, in theory at least, be identical. As large numbers of Mac users are finding out, however, that simply isn't the case.

Don't take my word for it – head over to Amazon and read some of the reviews for Dragon for Mac. Better still, check out the complaints at Nuance's own Mac forums. The software is currently in its sixth iteration, but things don't seem to be improving.

The program is generally riddled with bugs, some of which can cause things to grind to a halt or crash entirely. At a lower level, you will find common problems such as your cursor going walkabout, random letters inserted at the beginning and end of sentences and other characters appearing that you didn't dictate. The last update to version 4, for example, causes a crash upon exiting in OS X El Capitan. Nuance has since released Dragon for Mac 5 and Dragon Professional Individual for Mac 6, both expensive paid upgrades, yet the serious bugs in prior versions remain unfixed.

For Mac users, this can leave a bitter taste. The software is very pricey and can feel more like beta software than a finished product at times. That isn't to say the Windows version isn't without its problems, too, but it is generally a far more stable and reliable piece of software than the Mac equivalent. Just when the program seems to have been updated to the point of near-stability (e.g. version 5.0.5), the reset button is hit and Nuance release a new version entirely with all the bugs – and some new ones – back again!

The biggest problem with the Mac version, however, is in some core areas of functionality. Firstly, the ability to correct recognition results isn't as comprehensive as on the PC. You can add your own custom words to the program's vocabulary, just like in the Windows version, but Dragon for Mac has an annoying habit of ignoring your additions. The second big issue is with transcription. Being able to record your dictation on a dedicated smartphone or recorder is a fantastic tool and one we will explore in depth later in this book. If you own the Premium 13 version of Dragon NaturallySpeaking or Professional Individual 15, the transcription tool included works extremely well (note that the cheaper Home edition does not have this functionality) but the Mac version is extremely erratic in this area.

So if you are a Mac user and willing to put up with these issues (and why should you, giving you have paid for what should be stable, reliable software?), then go ahead and purchase the Mac version knowing its limitations. Alternatively, it may be worth considering running the PC version under macOS's Boot Camp or virtualisation software such as Parallels or VMware Fusion. This isn't an ideal solution, obviously, but you will probably save yourself the teeth-gnashing experience of getting the Mac software to work exactly how you want. After all, you want to write a novel not troubleshoot software, right?

Mobile Dictation

Almost everyone now owns a smartphone, tablet or even both. What many people don't realise, however, is that all of these platforms (whether it's Apple's iOS, Google's Android or Windows) have some form of speech recognition built-in.

For Apple users, it's Siri. Google has its own form of dictation, used in everything from searches to the Google Now assistant service. Windows, both on mobile devices and now on the desktop, uses Cortana. They all have slightly different functions and features, but the core usage is exactly the same – you can operate parts of the system using your voice, from looking for something on the web to adding a calendar entry.

What most people don't realise, however, is you can also dictate passages of text using all of these systems. For most people this involves simply speaking a quick text message or email, but it can be used for longer forms of writing, too – especially in something like Pages or Google Docs. Nuance provides the speech engine that drives Apple's Siri, so iPhone or iPad users may not realise it but a key component of Dragon is actually built in to their devices.

The big difference with using dictation on a mobile device is that the speech recognition is usually processed online. In other words, when you speak to your gadget, what you have said travels via your data signal to a server elsewhere and, in a split second, the results appear on your screen. This usually means that you can only dictate in short bursts of 20 to 30 seconds, but it's a good way to get used to using speech recognition in a casual manner.

In fact, if you are serious about integrating Dragon into your writing workflow, use your smartphone in this way as much as possible. Press the little microphone that pops up on your keyboard and dictate your emails, web searches and text messages whenever possible. Tap any words your smartphone gets wrong and be sure to correct them. This will at least provide some level of personalisation to your dictation accuracy.

Don't think of this as inconsequential – it is a vital part of your workflow. Using dictation in as many scenarios as possible, whether it's on your phone or at a computer, gets you used to the habit of speaking to an electronic device. A common area of difficulty that seems to hamper many people's use of dictation software is an unusual one – embarrassment. It's staggering how many times I've heard people say how silly they feel talking to a machine, yet they speak into their phone all the time. How would passers-by know if you're on a call or dictating a text? More importantly, why would they care? So what if you look silly talking into your microphone? You are probably never going to see the person looking strangely at you again!

In all seriousness, it's this development of a habit that is a fundamental part of gaining both comfort and confidence with dictation software. Once you become accustomed to the speed and accuracy with which you can perform simple dictation, you are likely to become far more enthusiastic about writing more complex, lengthy documents with the same methods. In fact, if your typing speed is something that has hampered you in the past then you are likely to find the sheer volume of words you are suddenly able to churn out in a relatively short space of time may turn you off typing completely.

Dragon is all about becoming comfortable with the process of dictation. The next section may be one that many non-technical types are put off by, but it can't be avoided. Once you have decided to make Dragon part of your life, you have to choose the hardware carefully that will help it to shine.

INSIDER TIPS

- Use your mobile device as often as possible to "train your brain" into becoming comfortable with dictation. Take advantage of Siri, Google Now or Cortana on your smartphone or tablet to dictate text messages, emails and perform searches.
- Consider your computing platform carefully – the Windows version of Dragon is significantly more mature than the Mac equivalent.
- If you are a Mac user or simply prefer that platform, consider running Dragon

for Windows on your device using Apple's Boot Camp software or virtualisation solutions such as VMware Fusion or Parallels. Bear in mind this will involve the extra expense of purchasing a Windows license to use on your Mac.

Part Two: Hardware - The Right Tools for the Job

It used to be so easy.

If you had dreams of writing a novel or were already a seasoned author, choosing hardware for the job was traditionally simple. Once upon a time we all used typewriters; those, obviously, have long since been superseded by computers. The choice of what to buy in order to apply your trade didn't require vast amounts of technical knowledge – in fact, even the cheapest of PCs were normally suitable. Writing has always been a profession that has relied more on the creativity, focus and time spent with your backside in a chair than the spec of PC you possessed. As long as you had access to a word processing program and a half decent keyboard, you had all the tools you needed.

That can still be true to some extent, but the way we work has changed dramatically in the last few years. Online features have now become essential parts of programs such as Microsoft Office and Google Docs. The days of simply buying a desktop or laptop computer are gone, with an emphasis now on being able to work anywhere on even the simplest of devices. This cross-platform interoperability combined with the advent of cloud storage has meant that you can now start working on a document on your desktop and pick it up later on your laptop, phone or tablet, right where you left off.

These considerations are equally important when considering your setup for dictation. Are you going to only dictate at your desk? If so, would you prefer a desktop microphone or a headset? If you also want to dictate while on the go, would you be better off with a laptop or convertible tablet of some kind? What about a voice recorder?

Don't worry. This may all seem daunting, but it's really not – it simply depends on how and where you want to work and making sure you pick the right equipment the first time to avoid unnecessary expense further down the line. We'll come to that later on in this chapter, but first let's concentrate on a vital part of the dictation puzzle that people so often get badly wrong – the microphone setup.

Microphones: Garbage In = Garbage Out

In almost every instance I've ever come across of someone who has had poor recognition performance from Dragon there has been a single, common weak point in their setup.

The microphone.

It goes without saying that Dragon can only understand what you feed into it. Voice recognition is a little bit like a dog riding a bicycle – it shouldn't even be possible in the first place, so don't be surprised if it looks ugly. The miracle of seeing whatever you speak transformed into text on your screen is a truly staggering technological achievement but it can only work properly if you are feeding it the best data you possibly can.

Nuance supplies microphone headsets with some versions of Dragon, both wired and wireless. They are almost always universally awful. I find it inexplicable that a company so keen on extolling the virtues of dictation and the accuracy of their product can provide something that results in such a terrible user experience out of the box. They are obviously intended as "getting you started" headsets, giving you the ability to use the product as soon as you've installed it. But the wired headset Nuance provides is very basic at best and I wouldn't bother even plugging it in. Factor in the cost of a better microphone and use that from day one.

I would also strongly recommend avoiding the version of the software that includes a wireless headset. Although this may seem a great convenience at first glance, the Bluetooth technology used simply isn't up to the task of providing highly accurate speech recognition results. Bluetooth headsets are generally fine for business tasks such as composing letters, emails and reports and controlling apps such as Microsoft Outlook. For long-form fiction writing, however, the technology simply doesn't provide good enough accuracy.

We'll cover this in more detail later, but it's probably best to accept that a high-quality wired solution is always going to give you the best results. If having a mobile, almost hands-free solution is important to you then there are better options such as voice recorders (again covered in more detail later).

So what constitutes a "better" microphone, anyway? Generally, it's anything that is specifically designed for high quality voice input – that could be a microphone normally designed for use in call centres or one that is suitable for podcasting or even vocals. That opens up a wider range of microphones than you might think and, again, the one you choose will largely depend on your personal preference. Would you prefer a headset? If so, choose a mid-price model like the Plantronics Blackwire series. These are specifically designed for telephone operator input and, as a result, have excellent noise cancelling qualities. This can make a big difference for speech recognition, especially if you are in an environment that isn't always whisper quiet.

If you are lucky enough to be able to dictate in peace, or maybe if you just don't like the idea of wearing a headset, desktop mics are also plentiful. The downside to these is that (surprise, surprise) you are tied to a desk in order to use them and their positioning and your distance from the microphone needs to remain reasonably consistent every time you fire up Dragon in order to maintain accuracy (and improve it over time).

In many cases, these can provide superior recognition to headsets due to the simple fact that they contain physically larger and better quality microphone components. Companies like AKG, Audio Technica and Blue make these microphones to capture high-quality music and voice – everything from singing to playing instruments to podcasting or audiobook recording. It goes without saying that the average musician requires high quality audio capture and, as a result, these types of microphone are well-suited to dictation.

The important thing is to choose the correct "pickup pattern". There are many terms – condenser, omnidirectional, dynamic and so on – in the microphone world that can be incredibly confusing, especially when all you want to do is get on with dictating. In a nutshell, if you are looking for a desktop microphone then pick one with a "cardioid" pattern. A good quality, reasonably priced example would be the Blue Snowball Ice (don't confuse this with the non-Ice version which is more expensive and includes pickup patterns that are not needed for Dragon).

This, like other cardioid microphones, excels at picking up the person directly in front of it, blocking out sounds from the side and behind. In order to pick up all the sounds in a room (for example, if you were conducting an interview or recording a lecture) you would want an omnidirectional microphone – but this would be totally unsuitable for dictation. Dragon wants to learn just your voice, not other voices around you!

A very popular microphone you may see mentioned a lot is the Blue Yeti. It's roughly twice the price of the Snowball Ice but has an adjustable pickup pattern, allowing you to switch from a cardioid setting to omnidirectional or even bidirectional (which will capture audio directly opposite you). If you plan to use your microphone for other things, like podcasting or recording music, then this is a good choice. However, don't pay extra for features you're never going to take advantage of. For dictation alone, these other settings are redundant so don't be deceived into thinking you need to spend more for the same level of quality.

A microphone such as the Blue Yeti is a great example of bang for your buck. It has plenty of additional features useful beyond dictation and offers outstanding clarity and quality for the price. Beyond this, though, things can get unnecessarily expensive. There is a law of diminishing returns when buying microphones – once you've hit a certain price point, usually around the $150 mark, you will simply be paying for features you don't need or marginally better components that make no difference to Dragon.

What if you don't want to use your microphone at a desk? You may be keen on relaxing on the sofa with your laptop by the side of you as you dictate your words. Well, you have the option of a headset again but this doesn't always provide the best quality. An alternative would be to pick up a Blue Icicle – this is a USB device that plugs into your laptop and allows you to use an XLR microphone, the type you see used by musicians on stage. Some of these microphones use something called Phantom Power in order to work, and the Blue Icicle will provide that. But there are plenty of good quality, affordable handheld microphones such as the AKG Perfection P5 that don't even require Phantom Power – just plug it in and start talking. Microphones like these are particularly handy when they have an "on/off" switch on the mic itself, enabling you to mute the input as you collect your thoughts.

The benefit of this latter setup is you get all the quality of the desktop cardioid microphone but with the portability of something you can hold in your hand.

One more thing – the connection you use is

important. You might have noticed that many microphones come with a 3.5 mm connection, similar to the one you find on your earphones. This is an old-school analogue connection and isn't always suitable for dictation. You might notice an awful lot of cheaper desktop and headset microphones have this, but you are likely to have poor results with microphones of this type as they are entirely dependent on the built-in sound card of the laptop or desktop they are plugged into. These are usually very basic sound chips, suitable for low-end audio only.

Make sure, therefore, that anything you use for dictation makes use of a USB connection. This removes your computer's built-in audio from the equation completely, whether it's a bridging device like the Blue Icicle or one of the desktop microphones named above. Oh, and that flimsy headset that came with your smartphone? Keep that for listening to music and making phone calls only. Dragon will not thank you for using it!

Anyone who's ever had poor recognition results in the past will probably find that if they had only spent a little bit more on a decent microphone they would have had significantly better accuracy. I know it's enticing to use what you already have or, having already spent a lot on the software, be tempted to make do with something cheap and cheerful. Please don't. It's obvious when you think about it that using a poor quality microphone for speech recognition isn't dissimilar to putting cheap, watery paint on your walls and expecting to get a perfect coat first time. It just isn't going to happen.

What about Wireless?

This has already been touched on, but it's impossible to talk about microphones for Dragon without going into more detail on the benefits and downsides of using a wireless setup.

On the surface of things, using a wireless microphone seems wildly convenient. Who doesn't hate having wires trailing and tangling everywhere? More importantly, a wired microphone means you are constantly tethered to your desk or wherever your computer running Dragon is stationed. A wireless headset eliminates this problem while giving you the ability to stand up and walk around more, something that can be both creatively energising and good for your general health.

Whenever people talk about wanting to get into dictation as part of their writing workflow, they invariably cite the health benefits as one of the reasons. After all, writing is a sedentary activity and, as I found out to my cost, it's not just repetitive strain injuries that a writer needs to worry about – there's also the horrors of developing back problems like I did or simply putting on weight from not getting enough exercise.

For any or all of these reasons, being able to cut the cord is an attractive prospect but, sadly, it's adding one more element of difficulty to a technology that is still only as reliable as the sound you feed into it. As we've previously mentioned, one of the main reasons people give up on dictation is because they aren't getting the accuracy they hoped for and the single most important way of countering that problem is to use a high quality wired microphone. That's right – *wired*.

Without spending vast amounts of money, there are simply no wireless microphones on the market that can provide anywhere near the level of audio quality required for the absolute best accuracy in Dragon. If you budget, say, £100 (or $150) to spend on a microphone, you will get a vastly better setup using any of the wired solutions we've already talked about. This kind of money simply doesn't buy you a wireless microphone that is going to provide anywhere near the same level of accuracy.

Bluetooth is quickly becoming the standard for wireless voice audio. There are all sorts of headsets available, from tiny ones that are barely noticeable to far more ostentatious examples with huge boom mics. They can also vary widely in price, from as little as £10 ($15) to five or ten times that, the more expensive models boasting "wideband" audio capture.

Sadly, even with the best possible Bluetooth headset, you are likely to be disappointed. Dragon is temperamental enough at the best of times and a Bluetooth microphone may be convenient but, as briefly mentioned earlier, it simply can't be recommended. Other wireless solutions using radio or DECT signals usually require the use of USB dongles and are equally compromised in some way.

I understand there are likely to be a lot of people disappointed by this – after all, it's convenient to be able to use a Bluetooth headset both with your dictation setup and for handling phone calls on your smartphone or via something like Skype. The only headsets I've found to work well with Dragon over Bluetooth are the Presence UC and the MB Pro 1 and 2, all from Sennheiser. These headsets use wideband audio (and you must always use the supplied Bluetooth dongles with them rather than your computers built-in chip), but they still require some tricky profile adjustments to work well, some of which simply may not be possible depending on your setup. Again, for the price you'll pay for these headsets, you will get a far better wired solution for a lot less money.

If you *really* want to move around while you dictate, consider using a handheld dynamic XLR microphone plugged into a Blue Icicle USB interface with an extra long cable – say, 3 to 5 metres (10 to 16 feet). This maintains an extremely high level of audio quality while giving you the flexibility to get out of your seat more often. It's not quite the freedom of a wireless setup, but it will provide significantly more consistent quality.

If you want complete freedom from wires then the best solution is transcription. We will go into it in far more detail later in this book, but adding a good-quality transcription solution to your setup gives you the freedom of wireless dictation without the compromises of wireless technology. It means adding a little bit more to your budget, for sure, but the results will be far better and you will end up with a comprehensive setup that covers you for dictation anywhere and everywhere, whether at your desk or out on a walk.

Choosing Your Computer

One of the great things about writing is that it is a truly universal profession. While, for the vast majority of people, computers have replaced typewriters or pen and paper, the barriers to entry are still extremely low. Technology has never been cheaper, with staggering amounts of perfectly capable, low cost computing devices flooding the market. It's now perfectly conceivable to pick up an inexpensive basic Windows laptop or Chromebook for less than £200 (roughly $300). Many have decent keyboards and free word processing software – whether it's Google Docs or a cut-down version of Microsoft Word – meaning everything a writer needs to start their novel is at their fingertips for very little money.

The same bang for your buck cannot be applied to Dragon, however. Inexpensive Windows tablets and laptops generally run on low powered processors like a Celeron or Atom and pack a measly amount of memory (typically around 2 GB of RAM). While there's no need to mortgage your house to buy a computer for the benefit of dictation, it pays to view what you are doing as an investment and spend a little more to get the best results possible.

Dragon is a relatively resource intensive program. It is, after all, taking a human voice and translating what you say into words on a screen – an incredibly processor and memory hungry task. Nuance claims that Dragon will work on relatively low spec hardware, but take those recommendations with a pinch of salt. One of the low-cost Atom PCs mentioned above will load up Dragon, for sure, but don't expect it to run well. If you have a decent microphone plugged in, accuracy won't actually be a problem – the recognition engine either works or it doesn't – but the speed with which your results appear on screen may be nothing short of painful.

This is where a beefier processor like an Intel Core i5 will work wonders. You don't need to stretch to an i7 unless you also intend using your computer for something like extensive photo or video editing. Pretty much any modern Mac or flagship Windows PC (such as the Microsoft Surface Pro, HP ProBook or Dell XPS lines) will have you covered.

You also need to consider both storage and memory (or RAM). A big 500 GB or 1 TB hard disk drive might sound tempting, but you would be far better off picking a computer that uses built-in SSD or flash storage. This will make everything feel significantly quicker and your programs, including Dragon, will load faster. 4 GB of memory should be a minimum – this is sufficient when using Dragon alone or with one or two other programs, but if you are the sort of person who likes having 20 tabs open in Chrome at the same time, you may want to consider 8 GB or more.

If you already have a computer, look at these recommendations and see how it stacks up. You may find that what you have is already perfectly sufficient, and any midrange Mac or PC built in the last couple of years should be more than capable. You may also be able to simply upgrade what you are already have (especially if it just means adding an extra stick of memory or changing your slow, spinning mechanical hard drive to a speedy SSD).

What could be more contentious is which platform you decide to settle on. We mentioned the differences between the Mac and PC versions of Dragon in chapter 1, and settling on one operating system or another is important. As someone who has used both Mac and Windows computers for most of my adult life, I have come to the conclusion that neither is better than the other. The Mac has traditionally had a more elegant, polished interface, although Windows 10 has done a lot to change that. PCs have always provided better value for money in many areas, yet mid to high-end laptops cost roughly the same from Apple, Lenovo, Dell or HP.

There are simply some things that Macs are better at and some things that PCs are better at. The Mac has always been the domain of the creative, excelling in things like audio production and video editing. Windows computers, on the other hand, have traditionally been synonymous with business software and productivity, with office software being a particularly strong point. But when it comes to word processing, neither platform is better than the other. Even Scrivener is available for Windows now.

When it comes to speech recognition, though,

my allegiances lie with the PC. As I mentioned before, Dragon for Windows is a far more mature and infinitely customisable piece of software than the Mac equivalent. That doesn't mean Mac owners should sell their computer and crossover to the other side – far from it. The Mac version will run just fine in most cases and you always have the option of using the PC version on your Mac via Boot Camp or software like VMware Fusion or Parallels. But if we are going to be honest about which is the best tool for the job at hand (which is, in this case, providing the absolute highest dictation accuracy possible) then a Windows PC is the best choice simply because the software Nuance provides is superior.

I sincerely hope that the Mac version of Dragon continues to improve and catches up to its PC counterpart in the future. In the meantime, be assured that there are workable solutions if you are an Apple user, even if that entails running the Windows software on your Mac. If you do decide to stick with the native Dragon for Mac version, then investing in a good quality microphone and following the guidelines for proper setup later in this book will go a long way to alleviating any shortcomings or problems in the software.

On the Go: Tablet Setups

The power of the cloud is one of the greatest advances in business productivity of our generation and we are still in its infancy. The days of being tied to a desk with a big, whirring PC tower underneath are gone (although that is still a good setup for a large amount of people). Laptops are getting thinner and lighter, yet they are not the only revolution in computer hardware we've seen in the last decade. It's hard to believe that, less than 10 years ago, tablets didn't exist. Well, that's not strictly true – they were around but they were slow, heavy and clunky. Worse still, those were their good points. The battery life was atrocious – sometimes less than two hours between charges.

Then, in 2010, everything changed. Apple introduced the iPad, a device (like the iPhone before it) that critics said wouldn't catch on. Even the name came in for ridicule from some quarters. Yet, as is usually the case, the critics were wrong and personal computing would never be the same again.

Tablets are an incredible leap forward in portable productivity, simply because they tend to be extremely lightweight and have exceptional battery life. They also tend to have better quality screens than a similarly priced laptop. There's just one problem with them – they don't have a physical keyboard.

The use of a keyboard case has become an easy fix to that particular issue, but things get more complicated if you want to use dictation as part of an extremely mobile, easy to carry tablet setup. I know plenty of writers who have at least two devices that they use at different locations and in different circumstances – a Windows laptop or MacBook, especially when editing, and a keyboard-equipped tablet or iPad when they just want to go to a coffee shop and get some words written.

If you're thinking of adding a tablet to your writing arsenal but want to use dictation, then you have to be honest with yourself before wasting any money. An iPad isn't going to cut it and neither is any Android tablet. The free built-in dictation on these devices is neither accurate or versatile enough to use as part of a consistent workflow. They also lack the ability to attach the high quality microphones we've talked about.

This is even true of the iPad Pro, Apple's flagship tablet released in late 2015. This has been marketed as a productivity device, complete with an Apple-designed keyboard cover. It has, however, exactly the same shortcomings as any other iPad. As it runs iOS and not macOS, you cannot use any desktop version of Dragon on it and, with only a single Lightning port for connectivity, you are out of luck when it comes to using pretty much any wired microphone on the market.

Only a Windows tablet will work in this regard, giving you both the ability to run the full Dragon desktop software and to plug in your microphone of choice. Again, there are some cheap Windows tablets which will do the job – *just* – but this is one area where you should be considering more of a hybrid device than a pure tablet.

Microsoft's Surface Pro 4 is probably the ultimate example of a truly portable, versatile platform for dictation. Dell also produce a professional tablet that will do a similar job in the Venue Pro series. Both of these devices prove that a tablet doesn't have to be a piece of companion hardware but can even act as your primary device, going from tablet to laptop and even to desktop (with the aid of a docking station).

Your preferences and budget are important, but consider this – do you want two devices with very different functionality such as a laptop and tablet, the latter of which cannot be used for Dragon? Or would you prefer one device that does it all, yet may not be as good at, say, the tablet side of things? Only you can decide, but bear in mind that if you do intend to use Dragon on a tablet device then your options are far more limited than for desktops or laptops.

If you are fully committed to using an iPad or Android tablet as part of your workflow, there is one solution – but it involves spending more money, in addition to the Dragon desktop software you may have already bought for your PC or Mac. Nuance have recently released Dragon Anywhere – a mobile app that brings the full power of the Dragon voice recognition engine to iOS and Android devices. At the time of writing (October 2016) it is only available in certain geographical territories, but these are likely to be expanded relatively soon.

This is the first and only genuine continuous dictation solution with the same promised level of accuracy as the desktop product on these devices. The catch? It's an ongoing subscription-only service, costing $15 per month or $150 per year for anyone interested. A major caveat is the need for a stable Internet connection at all times to use it and an inability to learn from your dictation in the same way the desktop product can. Over time, Nuance should continuously improve Dragon Anywhere – after all, they will want people to keep paying for a subscription, right?

It also circumvents the problems we've already mentioned with regard to the various versions of the desktop software and some of the installation and operating system compatibility issues people have experienced. Having said that, it remains to be seen whether this can be a truly viable desktop replacement solution or merely a companion app to the "real thing". Either way, it further indicates that there is a clear demand for speech recognition software and, in an era where we've grown used to asking Siri for directions or starting a sentence with "OK, Google", we are only ever more likely to see dictation products permeate the mainstream.

With this, hopefully, new entrants to the market will emerge and provide much needed competition in this space. Until then, Dragon is our one and only choice – so it makes sense when you are figuring out how to integrate it completely into your workflow, to choose your equipment wisely. Now we've gone some way towards that, it's time to finally get the software installed and start dictating. Get it right the first time and your results will be incredibly accurate from the moment you first start spinning your stories.

Microphone Setup

Whether you are using a desktop microphone or headset, something handheld or attached to the lapel of your shirt, one thing remains the same – you must treat your microphone with respect. If that sounds a bit melodramatic, I apologise – it is an inanimate object, after all. But don't expect your microphone to give great results, no matter how much you spent on it, if you are sloppy in the way you treat it. Remember that Dragon can only process what you say effectively if you have created conditions that allow it to do its job properly.

That involves adopting a consistent workflow when dictating. One of the most important things you can do is ensure that every single time you start to speak to Dragon, you are maintaining the same level of voice and distance from your microphone. This is essential for dependable, accurate recognition. With a headset, this is easy. Look in the mirror and adjust the boom microphone so it is approximately half an inch below the corner of your mouth. You don't want it too low or too high. Make sure that every time you place that headset on yourself in the future, you adjust the microphone to that exact same position.

What you are aiming for is uniformity. Even the slightest distance from a microphone can affect the results dramatically. This can be a little trickier with desktop or handheld microphones, but just make sure to put them in roughly the same position every time you dictate. It's going to become a habit – with any luck, you will simply repeat the positioning of both yourself and your mic every time you sit down to Dragon.

Adjusting your levels

When you first connect your microphone to your computer, you have no clue as to how loud or quiet the input is. This is one of the first mistakes people make when setting up Dragon – they simply plug it in and expect everything to work perfectly. And why shouldn't you? Things should be as easy as possible, correct?

Unfortunately, dealing with speech audio is an incredibly sensitive and complex operation for a computer to cope with. Although Dragon will do its own adjustments when you first start setting up the software, it is essential to make sure that the microphone you are using is loud enough and good enough quality in the first place. If you've gone out and bought something that can only provide pitifully quiet levels of input, you may as well return it and get something else. To find out what your sound levels are, you need a free piece of software called **Audacity** (you can download it from http://www.audacityteam.org).

Audacity may look complex when you first open it, but it's really not as scary as it seems. It's available for both Mac and PC and the interface is exactly the same on both – make sure your microphone is selected as the input next to the little icon and press Record. Talk to Audacity for a short period, maybe 20 to 30 seconds. All you are doing is a sound test, so you don't need to go on and on. When you are finished, hit the Stop button and play it back. Ideally, you should be wearing a pair of headphones or listening through good quality speakers when you do this as you won't be able to pick up the quality of the audio effectively from your tinny, built-in speakers.

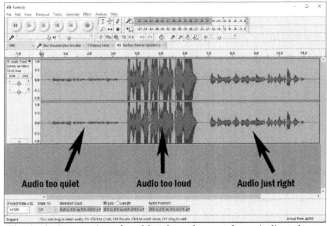

The Audacity user interface. Note how the waveforms indicate how loud or quiet your microphone input is. You need to aim for something similar to the right-hand side.

Listen carefully for tell-tale signs of poor quality audio. First things first – how loud is your voice? You want to be clear but not booming. The spiky lines on the audio recording you see shouldn't hit the very top of the waveform – this will indicate that your voice is "clipping", which is a fancy term for being too loud. Clipping audio will cause havoc in Dragon and is just as detrimental as being too quiet. To adjust the volume of your voice input to make yourself either quieter or louder, use the audio settings in your operating system to alter something called "gain".

On a Windows PC, right-click on the speaker icon in your taskbar and click 'Recording devices'. Select your mic, then click the 'Properties' button. You can now adjust your gain settings – don't forget to hit 'Apply'.

On a Mac, click the Apple menu (logo in top-left of screen) and click on 'System Preferences'. Click 'Sound' then "Input". Select your mic, then adjust the slider. Close when done.

It's very rare you would want to set a microphone to 100% gain. Somewhere within the 80 to 95% range is normal, depending on the sensitivity of your equipment. If your voice is too quiet, try moving your microphone nearer or sitting closer to it in the case of a desktop mic. If you're too loud, lower the gain or sit further away. If you are struggling with audio that is clipping badly from a headset mic, simply adjust the gain down. If your voice is too quiet with a headset mic, you may need to buy a different one as the position of the boom is obviously fixed.

Once you are happy with the level of your audio input, it's time to fire up Dragon and set it to start processing your dictation. There are some initial steps you can take to seriously improve the quality of your audio that most people know nothing about, so let's dive right in and get your accuracy as high as possible from the moment you start talking.

Initial Voice Calibration in Dragon

For the purposes of this section, I'm going to assume that you've already installed Dragon on your Mac or PC. The installation process is notoriously slow so go off and make yourself a cup of coffee or read *War and Peace* while you're waiting. I'm not kidding, it can seem as if your computer has crashed completely while you wait for Dragon to install. Goodness knows what it's doing, but trust the process and let it get on with it.

It may be a good idea to switch off any settings you have to put your computer to sleep while Dragon is installing and, if you have a laptop, make sure it's plugged in. There are many stories online of people who have had to wait upwards of an hour for the product to install on their system. I've never experienced anything that dramatic, but installation times of 30 to 40 minutes have been normal for me in the past.

If this is your first time installing Dragon, you will be creating a brand-new profile for your microphone setup. If you've already been using Dragon for some time, it is strongly recommended to discard the profile you've been using and start again with a new one based on your new equipment. This is because any recognition you have previously recorded will be based on a completely different audio input which may have been compromised by correcting words that would otherwise be recognised correctly with an improved setup. So whether this is your first time using Dragon or you are a seasoned pro, consider this a fresh start.

When you first create a profile, you will be given the option of selecting your age group, region and accent. Although the options can be quite general, try to make selections that are as accurate as possible.

I've found that Dragon works best with a standardised North American accent and, no matter how well I pronounce my British English, it still makes silly mistakes. If you are lucky enough to be from North America and speak clearly, you should get excellent recognition results off the bat, especially in the latest versions of Dragon which perform well out of the box.

For everyone else, you may have to accept a slightly lower rate of recognition with certain words. It certainly isn't enough to be a problem, but it's probably best to accept that once you have hit an extremely high recognition rate, it probably won't improve any further.

The key, then, is to get things as accurate as possible from the get-go. Once you have made these initial steps, you have an option to review your choices. There is a small "Advanced" button that allows you to choose the speech model Dragon uses.

Since version 12, Dragon NaturallySpeaking for Windows uses a recognition engine known as "Best Match V". This is designed for modern, powerful hardware and although most computers can cope with it admirably, you have the choice of dropping to an older recognition model if your resources are limited. If, for example, you are using a low powered Windows tablet or Ultrabook, or any machine with less than 8 GB of RAM, you may find better results by selecting "Best Match IV". Always make sure the "Vocabulary Type" is set to Large.

Both of the latest Dragon Professional Individual versions for PC (version 15) and Mac (version 6) introduce a brand-new recognition engine known as **Deep Learning**. This uses so-called artificial intelligence (AI) or "machine learning" to continuously improve your profile, even while you are using the software. Previous versions of Dragon required you to save your profile at the end of every session, allowing Dragon to load what it had learned the next time you used it. Deep Learning doesn't completely change this requirement, but it evolves it positively and adds this "on-the-fly" improvement. If you set up your profile to be as accurate as possible initially, you should see the new Deep Learning engine providing excellent results over time.

Whether you are using the Mac or Windows version of Dragon, the program will now go through the process of setting itself up with your microphone. When you are prompted to start speaking, **remain quiet for a couple of seconds before you utter your first words**. This is a vitally important and little known step to take that the program neglects to mention. That moment of silence enables Dragon to ascertain the "noise floor" of your microphone; in essence, the sensitivity of your sound input and level of background noise beyond the inherent noise of your mic itself. It is this **simple, virtually unknown** step that begins your process of creating a far more accurate setup.

When you are prompted to read text, speak at a normal pace and at a normal volume. Don't shout or rush through it. Imagine you are simply reading a book out loud – it is common to make the mistake of speaking at a higher volume than you normally would when dictating the first time you use a microphone. But we have already assessed our sensitivity in Audacity, remember? If you maintain that volume, you will be able to successfully dictate to your computer at a normal, low volume level. That doesn't mean you should mumble or whisper! Just speak as normally as you would when talking to someone.

Training Texts

Depending on your version of Dragon, you may or may not be presented after the initial sound test with a selection of texts to read. For v4 and v5 Mac users, you can't skip this step – simply select one of the options and follow the instructions, reading clearly and normally. In the Windows version of NaturallySpeaking or the latest Professional Individual for PC and Mac, you are not required to read any initial text.

Although Nuance recommends you read all of the training files at some point, there is little logic to this (even if the program pesters you to do it from time to time). This is because we want to train Dragon to learn our voice and, equally importantly, our *writing style*. There is no value in the program learning how you read somebody else's writing. The only time to use these texts is if you find recognition getting worse at some stage – but, to be honest, if that happens you are probably better off setting up a new profile again, anyway.

The same goes for the option Dragon gives you to scan through emails and documents on your computer. You should **never, ever allow the program to read through your emails** as it will include replies to *other* people's messages! Again, all Dragon will be doing here is reading someone else's writing style and that's not even taking into account the vast amount of spelling mistakes and abbreviations emails normally include. These sorts of documents are likely to seriously erode the accuracy of your profile and should be avoided at all costs.

Instead, feed Dragon a few of *your own stories* you have written. Print out, say, 2000 words of a story you have written and dictate it to Dragon. Make sure to correct any errors and, if necessary, save your profile. Repeat this exercise a few times. This is a far better way of training the program using a quick and dirty method to acclimatise the software to your writing style.

From this point on, you will be dictating your own writing to the program anyway and, if all goes as intended, your accuracy should continue to increase. The more you talk to Dragon, the more it learns not just how you speak but how you write. This is why those pre-installed training texts can do more harm than good.

INSIDER TIPS

- Choose a good quality wired microphone as part of your dictation setup.
- For portability, forget wireless microphones. They are expensive and generally inaccurate. Instead, use transcription to dictate on the go (we'll cover this in more detail later).
- Test and understand your microphone level in Audacity. You don't want a setting too loud or too quiet – use your computer's gain setting to alter this.
- When setting up a profile in Dragon for the first time, pause for a moment of silence during initial microphone setup. This helps the program ascertain how inherently noisy your microphone is.
- Ignore Dragon's prompts to feed it emails as these can damage your accuracy in the long run. Also, resist the temptation to read lots of built-in training texts as you will teach the program to learn your voice but ignore your writing style.

Part Three: Software – Training your Dragon

Congratulations! You've successfully set up your microphone and computer to start dictating effectively. Now it's time to become a Dragon power user – to get the software to not just put your words on a screen but to get them right with alarming accuracy. This next section will demonstrate how to tweak the program to give you the best results every time while adopting some of your own habits which will benefit you greatly in the long run.

This will include tempering your expectations of what speech recognition can achieve, of using tricks and shortcuts to quickly correct mistakes throughout your entire document and to harness the power of Dragon's built-in Vocabulary Editor. This tool alone can transform your workflow and, when used properly, enable you to format your document in your own style, saving valuable time during the editing process. Finally, this section will demonstrate how to set up additional microphones without impacting on any of the accuracy you've already built up in your profile.

First things first, though. We're going to start by adjusting our perception of what Dragon is for a writer by concentrating on its ability to help you put together a killer first draft. The editing comes later, along with all the other programs like Scrivener and Word that enable it. Right now we are going to focus on Dragon and Dragon alone, demonstrating how to ensure maximum accuracy by allowing it to utilise the full resources of your computer without overheads from other programs getting in the way.

Word vs Text Editors: Think First Draft

A common criticism levelled at Dragon is how erratic the program can behave in third-party software such as Microsoft Word, Apple Pages and OpenOffice or LibreOffice. No matter which version of Dragon I've used, I have always run into issues with one of these programs at some point. This can be anything from slow recognition to erratic cursor movements or even a blanket refusal from Dragon to operate in a particular program. If you have issues, spare a thought for Google Docs users – Dragon is virtually unusable for them.

Unless you are using Dragon for accessibility purposes (if, for example, you have mobility issues or rely on speech recognition to operate a computer), you have a far more simple option to increase both your accuracy and the stability of the program. If you've ever tried to correct something in the Mac version, for example, you will find that the cursor has to go on a journey to find the word or sentence you want to change in a program like Pages. This is due to restrictions with the operating system permissions within the program itself that prohibit Dragon from functioning normally. In other words, it *will* work but it's not without problems.

This problem has become especially apparent in the latest version of Dragon for the Mac, Professional Individual 6. Unlike Windows, the Mac operating system restricts how much access a program like Dragon has within other apps such as Pages or Word, partly due to security concerns. As a result, Dragon can appear to have a mind of its own and you can spend more time trying to get the cursor to stay where it's meant to be on the Mac than actually getting anything done.

As writers, however, we simply need to get as many words written as possible as accurately as we can. Why do we need to dictate in Word, Scrivener, Pages or any other program, anyway? When talking about word processors, Will Moyer once said: "The act of composing is about ordering and structuring thoughts. It's not about setting your margins or choosing fonts or italicizing phrases." This is so true - we're not even at the editing stage yet! Treat Dragon as an incredibly effective way to write your first draft and you can take advantage of another little-known trick.

Versions of Dragon for Mac before v6 opened a very basic text window with no formatting options upon start-up, known as DragonPad. The PC version of the program also has this which serves the same purpose (although it contains basic tools such as bold, italics, font styles and sizes etc). This is one area where I think the Mac version got it right; by using as little resources as possible in a basic text editing window, Dragon is able to concentrate on one thing and one thing only – accuracy.

Therefore, if you are a PC user, consider using Notepad for your dictation. This is a completely basic text editor built into Windows that takes up virtually no system resources. Depending on your setup, you may find your dictation is dramatically faster but, either way, you are releasing the burden of Dragon having to work within an already resource hungry program such as Microsoft Word.

For Mac users, your best option is currently to dictate into macOS's own TextEdit as, since version 6, the program has become notoriously unstable. Dictating into DragonPad in this instance (or even in previous Mac versions of Dragon) will cause you to lose your work in the event of a crash – sadly, if Dragon goes belly-up, it will take your work in the built-in editor with it. So, for the best balance of low resources and stability, use TextEdit. I would even go a step further and select *Format – Make Plain Text* to keep things as simple as possible. You can also turn this into your default format by selecting it in TextEdit's preferences.

Your results may vary, but I find that dictating into Notepad or TextEdit is snappier and makes correcting mistakes much faster. When you are done, simply copy and paste your text into your word processor of choice. As both TextEdit and the Windows Notepad lack formatting features, you will find pasting the plain text will allow you to format it however you want at the editing phase.

Your First Hurdle: Getting Used to Dictation

Let's be clear on this: dictation is an art. Some would also say it's an acquired taste, but we're not going to dwell on that. Because while writers will seemingly always find ways to either procrastinate or find any excuse not to use dictation, it has to be regarded as necessary. We've already talked about the benefits for your health and your word count, so isn't that reason enough? Besides, if you master the art of dictation then you give yourself the ability to write absolutely anywhere. We'll look at ways you can do that later, but for now it's important to focus on changing your mindset about dictation and how it relates to writing.

Writing is not typing. That's the first big misconception out of the way. I have lost count of the amount of writers – and I include myself in this category, on more than one occasion – who have told me that they simply can't use Dragon or any form of dictation as it doesn't feel natural to them. They talk of how a different part of your brain is required, how it feels soulless, *blah blah blah*. I'm going to be blunt here – these are excuses, and there is no excuse for making them!

Just like that other classic, "writer's block", there simply comes a time when you have to pull your big boy or girl pants on and get the work done. **Dragon is no different to typing**. There, I said it. It's just a different route to getting your words onto a page. Yes, there is some brain training to do. Specifically, you have to adjust to writing through your mouth instead of through your fingers. It can seem cumbersome having to dictate things like punctuation, but your brain does a little trick when you hit the quote, comma or period keys on your keyboard. You don't think of it when you do it, do you? The trick with dictation is to get to that point so talking feels as natural as typing.

Your first task is to write a throwaway story off the top of your head. Think of any topic, be it non-fiction or fiction, and just talk to your computer. Better still, close your eyes while you do it and ignore the screen completely. Seeing your words appear in front of you may be slightly magical but it's also fairly distracting, so cut that out of the equation right away and you'll put yourself in a better position in the future when you come to dictate while walking around or speaking into a voice recorder. There's no screen in front of you then, either, so it makes sense to form a habit that works straight away.

Don't worry at this point about story structure or anything even being remotely decent. All you are doing is getting words into Dragon so you can see how accurate your setup is and how much correction needs to be done. We'll call this the tuning phase – our equipment, if you followed the guidelines in the previous section, should be set up for optimal use. Now all we are doing is tweaking it to Dragon's liking.

Take a deep breath and have a glass of water handy. Your throat can get surprisingly dry when you are continuously talking. Start by writing something regarding your relationship with Dragon. Talk about how you feel about it, any challenges you envisage, and what you hope the outcomes will be. Make sure to throw a few complex words in there or things you particularly want Dragon to be able to pick up so if it gets them wrong, you can correct them at this stage. If you're feeling really brave, consider including some dialogue in there as well. It'll feel incredibly strange at first to speak every quote mark and piece of punctuation out loud. But stick with it – this is the ground work you will need to completely change your workflow for the better in the future.

Don't write more than 10 minutes' worth for your first exercise. When you've finished, copy and paste the text into Microsoft Word or another program that allows you to see a word count. How many words did you manage to speak in 10 minutes? Does the number disappoint or surprise you? Bear in mind that this is your first time dictating, so things will improve dramatically in the future. But if you can get even close to your typing speed at this point, you are going to see huge gains as time goes on. Once you are proficient with dictation and completely comfortable doing it, I would expect the average person to be able to write anything between 3000 and 5000 words an hour. For most mediocre typists (like myself), that's three or more times what I can achieve with typing, with none of the RSI or other health issues involved. Even for the fastest of typists, 5000 words an hour is nothing short of miraculous.

Make sure you correct Dragon on any mistakes it has made. You might be shocked, given how you set your equipment up, to find it's far more accurate than you would have expected. But, even if the results look good now, using the built-in correction facility will improve things by enough of a percentage going forward as to make a dramatic difference.

Speed vs Accuracy and Obsessively Saving Your Profile

Now that you have Dragon up and running and you've dictated your first mini masterpiece, it's time to head into the program settings and make some adjustments. In the PC version of Dragon, you will see an option to balance speed against accuracy. The slider is usually set in the middle of the range by default. If you are running the sort of computer that shouldn't be used for speech recognition at all, you would set this slider all the way to the left (for the fastest response). If you are running an absolute powerhouse of a computer, you can comfortably set the slider all the way to the right (to focus on the most accurate setting). In most cases, though, neither of these extremes are a good idea.

In my testing, trying to get the quickest response from Dragon simply makes too many errors and if you are using this option to mask the fact that your computer isn't powerful enough, it flies in the face of everything we are trying to achieve here. You have to accept that the software is reasonably demanding and invest in your equipment correspondingly, so trying to use Dragon on an underpowered system (the only beneficiary of this setting) is likely to prove an exercise in complete frustration.

On the other hand, selecting the most accurate option tends to make Dragon think a little too hard, resulting in slow recognition even on the most powerful of computers. I've also found that accuracy really doesn't get any better at this point than at the 60 to 75% mark, so you are simply wasting processing power with no improvement in results.

In truth, the best setting is usually four fifths of the way along the slider, between the centre and the extreme right hand side. On reasonably capable equipment, this provides an excellent compromise between acceptable speed and high accuracy.

While you are in Dragon's settings, make sure to select the option to automatically save the profile whenever you close the program. This means that any corrections you have made doing dictation will be saved to your profile when you exit the session. That way, you are always getting the most accurate, up-to-date version of your profile when you start up Dragon.

A quick note for Mac users: there appears to be a bug in Dragon Dictate for Mac 4 that crashes the program upon exit, resulting in your profile not being saved. This may not be replicable on all systems and I have mainly seen it in the latest version of macOS, El Capitan, but if you do encounter it there is a fix. Make sure to click the microphone symbol in Dictate to switch the mic off (don't just leave it asleep) before you exit. This seems to allow the program to exit normally and, since there do not appear to be any further updates coming to this version, will have to be used as a workaround. Versions 5 and 6 do not have this issue.

If you are using Dragon NaturallySpeaking for Windows, head over to the Data tab in the program's options. You will see a checkbox next to "Run Accuracy Tuning at the time scheduled by your Administrator". Uncheck this box. Nuance have employed various algorithms which improve the accuracy of your user profile over time; however, this is pretty much done on the fly. Every few saves, Dragon will prompt you to run Accuracy Tuning anyway, so there is no need to keep this option checked. This doesn't even exist in the Mac version – remember how we said earlier in this book how they were completely different programs merely using the same recognition engine?

You can also uncheck the option to "Collect Recognition Data". This adds to the processing load of your computer and, since you do not know what data is being sent, can be disabled purely for privacy purposes. On the Mac, this is at *Dragon menu – Preferences – Advanced – 'Send Anonymous Usage Data'*.

Just to clean things up even further, PC users should deselect these options again under "Tools – Administrative Settings". Also, select a folder other than the default for the backup copies of your user profile. Dragon will normally just save these on the same disk that the program is running from, which is useless in the event of a disk failure. You will lose both your profile and the backup! Set the backup copy to an external drive or synced cloud folder for safekeeping – this way, if you ever need to reinstall Dragon in case of a system crash or if the program itself just starts misbehaving, you will have a copy of your user profile elsewhere.

Training Your Brain, Revisited

Earlier in this book, I mentioned that it's a good idea to use dictation in as many different scenarios as possible, whether that's speaking into your phone to compose a text or email; or on your tablet or laptop to reply to forum posts or do a bit of blogging. I still maintain that this is a fantastic way to train your brain to get used to dictation fast. For example, I almost never search the web on my Android smartphone any more by typing. I just press the little microphone in the Google search bar on the home screen and ask Google to find what I'm looking for. This can be extended in lots of other ways, too. On your iPhone or Android smartphone (or your Windows phone, which uses Cortana, the same speech technology used on the Windows 10 desktop) you can ask your phone to do lots of different things, such as:

- Make an appointment at the doctors at 2 PM on Thursday
- What movies are showing near me?
- Navigate from Manchester to London
- Are there any good Italian restaurants nearby?
- Send an email to Joanna about the meeting on Tuesday
- Set an alarm for 7:30 tomorrow morning
- What is 42 feet 3 inches in metres?

By using your smartphone to perform everyday tasks via dictation, you become quickly accustomed to speaking to a machine. It can't be underestimated what an important mental leap this is. Think about how many people still don't like leaving messages on your voicemail – whenever you ask them why, they usually say it's because they don't like speaking "to those things"! Maybe I'm part of a slightly older generation that simply didn't grow up with technology in the same way a lot of young people now are. But I still feel there is a divide when it comes to your brain and your interaction with a computer. It's hard for it to feel natural, but it is something you're going to have to get used to if you want Dragon to work well for you.

When you interact with your other devices in the ways I've mentioned above, you will quickly find that you become increasingly comfortable with dictation in all its forms. You'll notice how, for example, even typing a text message to somebody is much slower than simply speaking it. Doctors and lawyers have used transcription for many, many years and Dragon's Medical Practice and Legal editions sell extremely well in these fields. If they can do it, why can't writers?

The simple answer is that we can, but we choose not to. There is a romanticism, it seems, associated with typing away at the keyboard and seeing the words translate into a story. But that romanticism is soon gone when you miss your own release deadlines because life gets in the way and you can't type fast enough to catch up. There's also nothing romantic about being crippled for months with a repetitive strain injury, not to mention the potential side-effects in the long term of being sedentary for so long, so much of the time. This was the lesson I learned when I had my serious back issues that I mentioned at the beginning of this book. I learned my lesson then and vowed never to make the same mistake again. It's one thing to not be able to earn money while you recover from an injury. It's another entirely to know that it was possible to have avoided it in the first place and, if you don't change your habits, it can rear its ugly head again.

Once you start to get used to dictation in other ways, like arranging your calendar or sending emails, dictating your fiction or non-fiction becomes much easier. That's not to say it won't still take a big period of mental adjustment, but you will find that all these little steps add up to a greater whole. In the end, it's about viewing dictation as another tool in your arsenal – even if you don't use it all the time (and nobody is saying you should), it's very likely that you will become enamoured with the ability to simply crank out thousands of words in half or even a third of the time it would take you to type. That becomes intoxicating pretty fast and the act of typing can start to be seen as a hindrance to your progression and workflow as a writer.

It's one thing to get used to Dragon or talking to a machine in general. But once you have become comfortable, then what? You should be getting to the point where your accuracy is pretty high, but there is still one more thing you can do to send things into orbit. It's something you can't do on those other platforms, like Siri, Google Now or Cortana. None of those tools, while useful, have the ability to learn a custom vocabulary – words and phrases that you use on a regular basis or even words that are already in Dragon's dictionary that you pronounce in a very specific way. Once you learn to harness the power of this incredible tool, you'll find Dragon can recognise exactly what you are saying as quickly as you can speak it.

Custom Words and Phrases

One of the major criticisms levelled at Dragon is that it isn't very good at recognising words and phrases that you might use in your writing but wouldn't be used in normal, everyday life. Whenever Nuance quotes figures of 99% accuracy for the product, I envisage thousands of authors foaming at the mouth when they seemingly get nowhere near that figure from their dictation. However, there is a very good reason for that.

It's easy to be frustrated by a product that says it can do one thing and delivers something else. But, as I've tried to show throughout this book, Dragon is a tool that you must learn to use effectively. If you are, for example, a science fiction or fantasy author or someone who writes stories with complex or unusual names or places, then there is a very good chance that Dragon is going to struggle with some of the words you are expecting it to recognise.

This is where you need to temper your expectations of Dragon and work with it instead of getting frustrated by it. Something tells me that the likes of George RR Martin would have a hard time expecting Dragon to flawlessly output some of the complex words used in his works. This is a good example of how you can adapt the program to work with you, not against you, in two very different ways. The first of these is to make use of the incredibly powerful Vocabulary Editor built in to Dragon.

In both the Mac and PC versions of the software, it's imperative that you always correct Dragon when it gets a word wrong. As you'll know through use, the program will present a list of words or phrases that it thinks are correct so you can replace the mis-recognised term with one that is more accurate. In Dragon for Windows you can also use the "Spell That" option if your choice isn't listed in the suggestions. This is one area where the PC version of the software differs from the Mac version and, in my opinion, this is a fatal omission from the latter. This very option (and the ability to train the software to the word you are correcting) is vital to the improved accuracy of the products and its absence for Mac users is one of the areas where, as I've already stressed, the macOS version will never compare as favourably.

However, both versions share a powerful Vocabulary Editor. You can access this from the training menu and this provides two incredibly useful tools. Firstly, you can look up any common word in Dragon's vast vocabulary (over 150,000 words, in case you're wondering) and train the software to your way of saying it. The methods for training differ slightly – on the PC, the program will ask you to speak the word only once; in Mac versions up to 5 you must do it three times (but only once in the new v6). In both cases, once you have trained Dragon to recognise your way of pronouncing that word, it should always be recognised correctly in the future.

This isn't the case with some words that Dragon will almost always struggle to recognise, however. These include mixing up *but* and *that*, *the* and *be*, and so on. No matter how many times you correct Dragon on these, it will always get them wrong from time to time. This is what I mean by tempering your expectations – just accept that these will always trip Dragon up like clockwork, and correct them manually. Don't bother training Dragon over and over to recognise your way of saying these very common words. It won't improve things. Concentrate on the much wider vocabulary and let those little words go!

Another area the Vocabulary Editor shines is when you want to train Dragon to always type a word in a certain way. For example, you can train the program to output a term like *Smashwords* correctly as long as you tell it the spoken form is *smash words*. This can be useful for company names, place names or anything that you want capitalised.

What about those complex character or place names, however? Well, this is where it probably pays off to just accept Dragon's limitations and stop expecting it to perform miracles. The thing is already taking your voice and turning it into words on the screen, for goodness sake! If you are writing about a character called Araghnya the Destroyer who lives in the Kingdom of Omipotamal, simply call her Jill from the Kingdom of Manchester and use the 'Find and Replace' function in your word processor of choice to sweep through your document and make those changes manually later.

Remember, we are trying to develop a first draft as quickly as possible. You can use the Vocabulary Editor to train Dragon to always recognise those names and complex places, of course, but it is usually a futile exercise. It may get some right, but will often get many wrong. Don't do anything that is going to put you off using the product when you get frustrated at a lack of accuracy beyond what you can reasonably expect.

Don't forget - the editing phase is the time when you can add in all of those complex custom words using the Find and Replace function. Make it your priority to get your words into a completed first draft. By employing a little bit of common sense, Dragon can help you achieve this in record time.

INSIDER TIPS

- Use a program like Notepad for Windows with low system overheads to increase accuracy in Dragon (the Mac version uses its own built-in app like this by default up to v5; for Mac v6, use TextEdit in Plain Text mode).
- Think first draft – you do not need to edit at this stage, so avoid using bloated software with formatting tools while dictating. Your only aim at this point is to write as many words as

possible as accurately as you can.

- Use the Vocabulary Editor within Dragon to add custom words and phrases as well as names of people and places. You can also train Dragon to recognise the way you say any word that is tripping it up.
- Make use of the 'Find and Replace' function within your word processing program during the editing phase to replace placeholder names with those of the actual characters or locations in your story. Don't expect Dragon to consistently recognise very complex words or phrases – use this shortcut instead to ensure your dictation sessions simply generate as many words as possible.

Part Four: Next-Level Dictation

Consistent Accuracy Anywhere, Anytime

Take it from someone who knows – writing can be a solitary, lonely profession.

One problem with spending so long sat in a room, hunched at a keyboard and staring at a screen is, apart from the obvious repetition, the loss of human contact. It can be miserable. There's nothing worse than staring out of the window, watching the world go by, while you sit indoors desperately trying to finish the first draft of the novel you promised yourself you would have had ready to edit by now.

That's why it makes sense to get out of your house, office or wherever else you normally write and change your location now and again. One of the benefits of using Dragon is that it can free up time to do other things – go for a walk, a cycle ride or even just chill out for the afternoon. But what if you want to turn that time into something productive as well? What if you could dictate a thousand words or more, simply while you are popping to the shops or walking the dog?

And what happens when you want to *really* change your environment? You might decide to work in your normal space during the morning then relocate in the afternoon to a coffee shop, co-working space or library. Those places make it tricky to dictate in, due to the amounts of other people nearby, yet they are also essential environments for human contact, even if you're just people-watching and getting some fresh air or a change of scenery.

It's never been easier to work on the move. With access to an Internet connection, even if it's just tethered from your mobile phone, a writer can pretty much open their laptop and start creating their next story anywhere. And don't think that you can't dictate when you want to spend an afternoon at a coffee shop – you may not want to talk out loud or might even feel conscious doing it while you are sitting with your Flat White, but that doesn't mean you can't use that time to import words you have already dictated. You could even have written thousands of words on the way to the coffee shop – try beating that for productivity!

In this section, we are going to explore the options available for setting up multiple microphones with your Dragon profile. We are also going to look into what I believe is the ultimate way of dictating – using a voice recorder and harnessing the power of Dragon's built in transcription tools so you can, quite literally, dictate anywhere and anytime. The point of this section, however, isn't just to give you ideas on how to set up these things – the goal is to ensure your profile remains as accurate as possible, giving you consistent levels of recognition no matter which type of microphone or location you are in.

A Mic for Every Occasion

Despite what many people may think, Dragon does not require an absolutely pristine audio environment. There's no need to build yourself a booth with foam padding on the walls, similar to the types of things you would find in a recording studio. You're not doing voice-over work for a television documentary, you're just trying to get some words on a screen!

That being said, the *'Garbage In = Garbage Out'* rule that we talked about earlier in the book still applies. There are many good quality headset and tabletop microphones with noise cancelling properties, so if you aren't in the quietest of environments, don't worry. Obviously, any extraneous sound should be avoided if only because it makes it more difficult for you to concentrate. But think about how noisy a call centre is. Very often you will find that when you call someone for customer service you won't hear any other voices in the background. This would indicate that those particular environments are using high quality, noise-cancelling headsets. It's these sorts of things that you can also use effectively for Dragon.

Wired versus wireless is something that people will continue to debate. Don't get me wrong, there are some very good quality wireless headphones out there but they tend to cost a fortune and you would be likely to get equally good, if not better, quality from a wired microphone costing a tenth of the price. For portability between locations, it's tempting to go wireless but, reiterating my points from earlier in the book, I would steer clear of it and consider Bluetooth technology a complete no-no for speech recognition.

Instead, think very carefully about the environment you are going to dictate in and choose your microphones accordingly. For wired flexibility, a USB-powered Blue Icicle adapter gives you the choice of using any handheld microphone with differing cable lengths that have XLR connections. This can prove fiddly, though, as you will have to transport all the various bits you need to get a dictation session started. You will need to plug in the USB cable, then the Blue Icicle adapter, then the microphone cable, then the microphone itself…

Instead, think about whether you would

really be happy with this sort of setup involving adapters and analogue audio connections. For the vast majority of people using speech recognition on a computer, a USB powered microphone is always going to be the best bet. It's a universal connection and, as always, it's the microphone that provides the quality of speech input, not the type of connector. At your home or office desk, you may prefer a desktop microphone like the Blue Yeti, Audio Technica AT2020USB or Blue Snowball Ice that we mentioned earlier in the book. Just remember to pick something with a cardioid pickup pattern so that when you sit in front of it and speak, external sounds are blocked out.

When you pick up your laptop and head out to the coffee shop, things change. You certainly don't want to be trailing around with a heavy desktop mic in tow. Instead, choose a tiny but high quality microphone like the Samson GoMic. This clips on to the top of your screen (or can be placed on a desk) and has an excellent quality cardioid pickup. Alternatively, plug in a noise cancelling USB headset such as the Plantronics Blackwire series. These are both great options depending on your preference, but what if you don't want to be dictating in another location with people around?

Your choice then becomes far more simple than you may realise. It involves doing your dictation on the go – whether sitting down on a park bench or while you are out walking. To capture your voice in an audio file, you have two good options – either a recording app built into your smartphone or a dictation machine. The former depends on how good the microphone is on your particular smartphone; the latter is inexpensive and provides a dedicated device with phenomenal battery life.

By using your change of location to then import the files you have created and edit them, you are not only getting away from your regular desk but are also using the time it takes to move from one location to another effectively. One thing I do recommend, though – set up your computer's internal microphone as part of your Dragon profile. I don't recommend actually using it – the internal mic even on a good quality laptop is usually of insufficient quality for accurate speech recognition. But it's important to have it set up, purely so that if you want to fire up Dragon to import your audio files for transcription and you do not have your regular desktop mic or headset attached, the program will actually open! If you only have your profile set up for an external microphone, Dragon won't proceed until you plug it in. By having your internal microphone set up as well, even if you never use it for actual dictation, it enables the program to open up correctly as the internal microphone is always present.

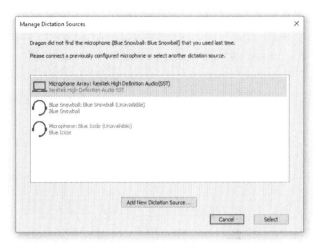

When opening Dragon away from my desk, the program cannot find either of the Blue mics I normally use. By adding my internal mic (top option), I can select it and still use the program to import transcribed files. Use 'Add New Dictation Source' to achieve this.

The next section is an important one. It focuses on transcription – using those audio files we just talked about to pull your words into a Dragon produced document. For many writers, transcription could be the thing that really turns them on to dictating. It doesn't involve having to sit at the desk for hours at a time, doesn't require wearing headsets or using complex XLR to USB microphone setups, and it enables you to dictate your writing pretty much anywhere.

It also takes the pressure off looking at a screen and disrupting your flow by correcting Dragon when it makes mistakes. Those things can be reserved for later – the editing session in the coffee shop, for example. The choice becomes not whether to use transcription, but how to do it and what equipment to use for maximum effectiveness.

Transcription: the Holy Grail of Dictation

My job isn't to convince you to use dictation as part of your writing workflow. Hopefully, merely by picking up this book in the first place, you've already decided this is something you want to do and have embraced the possibilities it holds. Nevertheless, there is one area of dictation that I get genuinely enthusiastic about more than any other, and that is transcription.

Once upon a time, transcription involved talking into a voice recorder, giving the file to somebody to turn into a typed document and handing over vast sums of money in the process for the privilege. Transcription can be very, very expensive when a human is involved. Think about it – how much would it cost to get someone to type up an entire novel? Now multiply that by your second third and fourth novels and you could soon find yourself paying out huge amounts for a transcription service.

Thankfully, nobody needs to do that anymore. Until a few years ago, the ability to transcribe a recording directly into a computer was the stuff of science fiction. As if talking into a microphone and seeing your words appear on screen isn't incredible enough, being able to dictate at any given time and in pretty much any location is an even greater step forward. It frees you from the computer entirely; you don't need one with you when it's time to dictate at all. You simply store up your recordings, feed them into Dragon when time or convenience allows, and let the program do the rest.

Despite the incredible capabilities of the program, however, this feature is a relatively new phenomenon to the masses. Incredibly expensive versions of the software (for example Dragon Medical and Legal) provided this facility in the past, but this was very specialised and cost prohibitive for most people. Since version 11 of Dragon NaturallySpeaking for Windows, however, the "Transcribe Recording" function has been present for anyone to use as long as you bought the Premium version of the program. That's still true for the most recent versions and, as a result, is one reason I would never recommend the Home version. It lacks this vital time-saving feature and it's likely to be something you will want to use all the time once you've tried it out.

Mac users have had this feature since Dragon Dictate version 4. Both Dragon for Mac 5 and Dragon Professional Individual for Mac 6 also have transcription features which bring it more into line with the Windows equivalent.

The question is: how do you get your recordings into Dragon in the first place and how do you ensure the same level of accuracy you have achieved with your microphone setup? It's a lot easier than you think and, if you have *at least* Dragon for Mac 4 or NaturallySpeaking version 13, pretty straightforward. I wouldn't recommend purchasing versions of the program below these unless you are running an older operating system and have no intention of upgrading. Version 12 (upgraded to 12.5 with a patch from Nuance) has notorious problems installing under Windows 10 and I've also experienced issues with it in Windows 8.1, though you may have better luck. Anything below version 4 for the Mac does not work with macOS El Capitan, and even then it's a little flaky. Nuance obviously wants you to update to the latest Dragon for Mac 6, but I have had success with version 5 (with the latest Nuance patch to 5.0.5) in the most recent version of the Mac operating system, Sierra.

There are two main options for transferring your dictated audio files into Dragon. The first is to record them using a smartphone. Virtually every modern phone has a built-in voice recorder app and, if yours doesn't have one or isn't suitable (we'll get to that in a minute), you can normally download one from either the iOS App Store or the Google Play store. The most important thing on a phone, however, is not the app that you are recording in – that can be fixed by using a different one. As with the considerations for desktop or headset microphones, the quality of your phone's built-in mic is the primary consideration.

If you are using a relatively high end smartphone such as an Apple iPhone, Samsung Galaxy Note/S6, Nexus 6P, Huawei P8 or LG G4, you will probably find that all of these phones are highly suitable for voice recordings. You can even download free apps such as Smart Voice Recorder that allow you to tweak your input levels and quality settings accordingly.

Sadly, most smartphones (especially lower end Android and Windows phones) don't tend to have good enough microphones to give adequate results for speech recognition. This is purely down to the level of miniaturisation in a phone and the cost of the components used. It's a miracle how tiny the microphones in these devices are to begin with, but when you are using a smartphone that is relatively inexpensive, you will find that the internal microphone is often very basic.

If you don't have an expensive smartphone or don't want one, there is an excellent – and, some would say, better overall – solution. For a relatively low price, you can buy a dedicated voice recorder or dictaphone. Whether you decide to go the smartphone or voice recorder route, you must ensure that the app or device you are using can record in a format that Dragon will understand. These are as follows:

Dragon for Windows can import .wav, .wma, .dss, .ds2 and .mp3 files.
Dragon for Mac can import .aif, .aiff, .m4a, .m4v, .mp4 and .wav files.

A WAV file is a format typically used for uncompressed LPCM audio, meaning there is no loss of quality in the recorded file; this, however, results in a very large file size. If you are recording on a smartphone such as the 16 GB Apple iPhone, which has low built-in storage and no option for an additional memory card, this could prove problematic although you would have to record a fair amount of audio before you fill it up. As a guide, 60 minutes of dictation in uncompressed WAV format will result in a file around 300 MB in size (1000 MB = 1 GB); an MP3 or M4A file of the same length will typically be around 4 to 6 times smaller.

Many voice recorders have built-in memory but most now also have a microSD card slot. This enables you to not only record to a virtually unlimited amount of storage (as you can just swap out the cards as needed) but also gives you a way of easily transferring your files to and from a computer without having to deal with USB cables.

Another advantage of using a smartphone is

that you can simply upload your recorded file to your cloud storage provider of choice, such as OneDrive, Dropbox or Google Drive. If you have set up your computer to sync with this, you will find your file ready and waiting for you almost as soon as you switch your PC or Mac back on. It's then an easy process to simply import the file into Dragon from the storage location – no cables, no connections, no fuss. As slick as this may be, however, it is obviously dependent on an Internet connection and a reliable cloud service. Alternatively, you can simply transfer your files the old-fashioned way with a USB cable.

A major disadvantage of using a smartphone for your audio recordings is battery life. Although you can set your screen to turn off after a certain amount of time, this can be a pain when you are recording audio files for transcription. You often want to pause and collect your thoughts, and if your screen has been switched off you then need to unlock the phone to get back to the recording app's user interface. This isn't a problem on a dictaphone, where you can simply hit the record button to pause it and press it again to resume. Leaving the screen on while you record on a smartphone is likely to sap the battery life quickly on a device which is already challenged in this area.

This highlights one major advantage of using a dedicated voice recorder instead of a smartphone. All the devices you are likely to come across will have exceptional battery life – they usually operate on one or two AAA or AA batteries, are incredibly light to carry around and will likely take months of recording before a battery switch is required. Even when that happens, there's no need to charge anything – you simply put in a new, standard set of batteries (be aware, there are some voice recorders such as the Philips DVT4000 Voice Tracer which have rechargeable internal batteries and you must decide whether you are comfortable with this feature before purchasing).

The other major advantage of a voice recorder is that it is simply very good at what it does. It is a dedicated, single purpose device. The microphone used is likely to be of a relatively high quality and tuned precisely for voice capture. You will also find inputs on many models for external microphones, such as a lavalier (aka 'lapel') mic to attach to your shirt or collar. This can be particularly handy if you want to record some dictation while you are out and about walking. Just attach the Mic to your clothing, put the voice recorder in your pocket and press the record button. Bear in mind that a good quality lavalier mic is infinitely better for speech recognition than the sorts of in-line mics found on some phone headsets.

When it comes to purchasing a voice recorder, don't spend more than you need to. Dragon does not care about stereo recordings, so fancy dictation machines with more than one on-board microphone are a waste of money. You simply need something that provides good, reliable mono recordings. Also, look again at the file requirements in the section above. The most common file used across both Mac and PC platforms is MP3 – this is a compressed audio file, but if you record at 192 kb per second, usually the highest setting available for MP3 on a voice recorder, you will find the quality to be more than sufficient. I have seen no accuracy difference between a 20 MB, 15 minute MP3 audio file recorded this way and a 75 MB WAV file of the same length. The accuracy, in both cases, was identical.

If you absolutely *must* have the maximum quality possible from your voice recorder or smartphone, record in WAV at 44.1 kHz (44100 Hz, CD quality) if it allows. Try making two recordings of the same length and complexity using both WAV and a compressed format (at best quality settings) in MP3 or M4A. Run both files through Dragon and see if you notice any drop in recognition accuracy; if not, stick with the compressed format, especially if storage capacity on your device is an issue.

Again, this is the law of diminishing returns. Don't scrimp on a cheap, low quality dictation machine – if you decide to go down this route, there are plenty of excellent quality models from the likes of Sony, Philips, Olympus and Panasonic. A budget of £50/$75 is probably the most you should spend; beyond this, you are simply paying for features (like extra microphones and pickup patterns) that you don't need.

Some quick and dirty tips for getting good quality audio files for Dragon to transcribe:

- Set your audio quality to HIGH (usually 192kbps or above) and in MONO;
- Set your microphone sensitivity to LOW (to avoid audio clipping);
- If there is a "Low Cut" setting, switch it ON;
- If there is a "Noise Cut" level, set it to "Maximum";
- Switch "Noise Cut" ON if you have it when dictating outdoors or in noisy conditions. At all other times, leave it OFF;
- If your recorder has an LED indicator, switch it ON so you can quickly see when you are recording or paused.

Using a voice recorder, whether on your smartphone or with a dedicated voice recording device, is an incredibly liberating way to dictate your books. You are almost certainly guaranteed to be carrying your smartphone with you everywhere you go, so this will always be a good option. But a dictaphone is also more than small enough and light enough to keep with you at all times as well. This way, if you are out on a walk, waiting for a bus or train, or simply sitting in the car you can write pretty much anywhere. Once you get used to this way of dictating without a screen in front of you to constantly divert your attention and cause you to make corrections, you will find yourself getting used to dictation very quickly. Transcribing the files later in Dragon when maybe your creative juices aren't flowing as much is also a great way of managing your time.

A quick word of warning, though – Mac users may find that while the transcription function in their version of Dragon is convenient, it will simply never be as accurate as in the PC equivalent. This is because the latter allows you to correct mistakes in the transcribed text after it has appeared on your screen. On the Mac, however, this isn't possible – text is simply output to a Word or RTF file with no ability to correct it (other than manually via the keyboard, of course). If you cannot correct with your voice, then Dragon cannot learn. As a result, your transcription accuracy can never significantly improve on the Mac whereas you should be able to get your transcription profile on a PC to the same level of accuracy as your normal dictation profile.

One thing is for certain – using transcription whenever and wherever you have a spare ten or fifteen minutes to dictate will see your word count piling up in no time. When you feed those files into Dragon later on, you may shock yourself at the sheer number of words you've been able to achieve by simply pulling out a voice recorder when you had a spare few minutes in your day.

INSIDER TIPS

- Once you have set up your profile and it is providing good accuracy, add any other microphones you will be using to Dragon. Ensure they are of equal quality and their gain levels have been properly set using Audacity and your OS sound settings.

- Add your internal laptop or tablet microphone to your Dragon profile but don't use it for dictation. This is purely so you can open the program and import transcribed files when you are on the move.

- If you intend to use transcription, decide whether to use a smartphone or voice recorder. The phone will need to be of a relatively high quality with a decent internal microphone. Bear in mind that using this for dictation will impact your battery life; a separate voice recorder overcomes this but means carrying around an additional device.

- Consider using a cloud storage service such as OneDrive or Dropbox to upload your transcription files direct from your smartphone. This eliminates the need for cables and your file should be sitting on your computer, ready to import to Dragon almost as soon as you switch it on.

- If you intend to buy a dedicated voice recorder, pick one with a USB port and microSD storage. This not only gives you increased capacity but allows you to connect the whole device to your computer to transfer files instead of constantly taking the small, easily lost card in and out.

- Ensure any device you use for transcription records in the formats your version of Dragon will accept. If you are set on recording in uncompressed WAV format, both the Mac and PC software will accept this but remember that the file sizes will be much larger.

- Do not pay for features you do not need. If you have a good quality smartphone, you can pick up an app for very little money (or even free, such as Smart Voice Recorder for Android) that will give you the ability to adjust the settings for your recordings. This should be all you need. If, however, you intend to buy a voice recorder then stick with one with the basics – paying more for stereo microphones, for example, is a waste of money as Dragon will not take advantage of them.

Part Five: Off and Running

Congratulations. By this point you should be a fully fledged dictator – in a good way!

Now that you've figured out how to use dictation in a way that can transform your writing workflow, it's important to reiterate some points we've covered in this book. In short, these are the things you must do in order to make Dragon work for you and deliver the highest level of recognition accuracy possible.

Invest in Both Software and Hardware

There has to be an acceptance that in order for Dragon to work well, it's not enough to just buy the software and install it on any old computer. You will need a relatively modern PC or Mac and, more importantly, a good quality microphone. I've seen so many people balk at the price of some of the microphones we've covered in this book, yet is $65 to $125 (around £50 to £100; the Blue Snowball can be bought for as little as $50) really too much for what you are getting?

How much did your MacBook cost? Or, if you

use an Apple desktop computer, how much would it cost to replace your shiny aluminium keyboard? You guessed it – about $100. All good quality kit costs money, so accepting that there is an amount you need to *invest* in your career, not just spend, is important.

Nuance publish recommendations for microphones and voice recorders on their website that they recommend to use with Dragon. Take these with a pinch of salt – many of those products are out of date or impossible to find; for many others, there is no explanation as to why they have achieved a certain rating from Nuance. For example, Nuance recommend several versions of the Philips Voice Tracer recorders which have stereo microphones and, in some cases, no option for mono recording. These recommendations make little sense when Dragon has no need for this sort of hardware. Go back to basics – if you use something specifically designed to capture the human voice clearly and cleanly, you will get good results with Dragon on the whole.

Consider Your Workflow

Do you use a Mac or a PC? Do you write in Microsoft Word, LibreOffice Writer or Scrivener? The other elements of your writing workflow are important to consider as Dragon is only a tool that will enable you to quickly get a clean first draft. If you are comfortable having multiple computers, like a desktop and laptop, then consider that in your budget and remember that if you want to use Dragon on both, you will need to install it on two separate machines and maintain the user profile on both. Also, the licence for the Windows version of the software does not cover the Mac version and vice versa – so if you are thinking of mixing platforms, this will prove more expensive.

Maybe you would rather use only one computer, such as a laptop, that you then dock to a large monitor at your desk. In this case, the decision is more simple but still involves considering whether you want to use the Mac or PC version of the software. As we've discussed earlier in the book, Apple users are stuck with what I consider to be a substandard version of Dragon, even though the recognition accuracy is initially good.

If you would prefer a device that does it all – taking you from tablet to laptop to desktop – then something like a Microsoft Surface Pro 4 would fit the bill. This would give you one version of Dragon with one user profile that you can use across all scenarios. But bear in mind that, with the use of a voice recorder, you can dictate anywhere and everywhere at any time and import it later so having multiple platforms or devices shouldn't be a concern.

It all comes down to your personal preferences and budget. Consider these carefully as you will be committing to a workflow that you will hopefully be using for a very long time to come.

Perfection Is the Enemy of Progress

I recently heard a quote that struck me – "done is better than perfect". I can't remember who said it but kudos to the knowledge on display in those five simple words. When it comes to your writing, the biggest hurdle is just getting the words down on a page. The next brick wall is actually finishing your manuscript and, as it happens, Dragon is perfect for this very purpose. It's an ideal tool and, hopefully, one you will find indispensable for simply completing a first draft.

The temptation to continually correct Dragon on every little thing it gets wrong and expect it to deliver 100% accuracy all the time is futile. Who cares if it gets "the" and "be" mixed up almost every time? Fix it in editing. Why does it matter if it can't remember the incredibly complex character names in your science-fiction novel? Fix it in editing. Why do you need to insert bold in a heading or italics during a section of dialogue? Fix it in editing.

By using placeholders for complex character or place names and the Find and Replace tool in your word processor, you can concentrate on one thing and one thing only – getting your first draft done. Work within the limits of Dragon and accept that a certain level of accuracy is more than enough. No matter how hard you try, Dragon will never get certain words correct. Accept that and move on. For the vast majority of people, once you have hit an extremely high level of accuracy (anything above 98%) you will almost certainly be putting up with only as many (or even fewer) mistakes than if you were typing! I don't know about you, but I am a horrible typist and Dragon certainly makes far less mistakes than I do. You also never have to worry about misspelling a word again! This is one of the hidden advantages of using Dragon – your spelling is 100% perfect, every time.

Don't Train the Software to Learn Things You Didn't Write

This one is controversial, I know, but I'm going to repeat it as I can't stress enough how important it is. The software encourages you to read training texts so it can learn your voice and improve accuracy. But from all the research I've done and the people I've spoken to who work within the speech recognition field, this is a pointless and potentially damaging exercise. Beyond initial recognition, you should not train Dragon to learn things that you have not written. It's vitally important to remember that Dragon doesn't just learn how you speak, it learns how you write. By reading someone else's work, you are messing with the very algorithm that is designed to make your voice as accurate as possible when you use the product. Remember, this also goes for feeding the program documents such as emails – as we mentioned earlier, don't do this as those emails will contain other people's writing (and bad spelling!).

Think about it. If you've followed all the steps in this book, you should be achieving 98% to 99% accuracy. That's just one or two mistakes in every 100 words – a phenomenal level of recognition. How many typos do you make for every 100 words? How is training Dragon using the built-in exercises going to improve things any further? The simple answer is that it won't. Dragon will now continue to learn your voice and your writing style on-the-fly. When it makes mistakes, you will correct it. There is simply no need at this stage to sit for 15 minutes and dictate passages that didn't come from your brain.

The only time reading those texts can ever be

justified is for initial voice calibration and if your profile starts to degrade – in other words, your accuracy starts to dramatically drop. But in that latter case, I would argue that it's simply best to create a new profile from scratch. Once a profile goes downhill, no amount of training can usually save it. Something has usually gone fundamentally wrong in your setup – maybe you introduced a new, poor quality microphone that has completely screwed up Dragon's recognition of your voice. Either way, simply export your custom vocabulary so all your words and phrases you added to the built-in Vocabulary Editor are intact, create a new profile and import them back in. Things should be as good as new.

Use the 'Import list of words or phrases' option under the Vocabulary menu in Dragon to keep your customised words from another profile. A similar option is present in Dragon for the Mac.

Write in Bursts and Embrace Transcription

Once you start to dictate regularly, you'll be surprised at how tired your voice gets. There's a difference between speaking to a person in conversation and dictating to a machine. You tend to keep a fairly monotone voice and, before you know it, you will find your throat getting dry. Keep a bottle of water on hand and try to dictate in bursts of maybe 15 to 20 minutes at a time. This gives you a chance to recharge your batteries before diving back in to do another session.

Just two or three 20 minute dictation sessions throughout the day could generate as much as 1000 words *each*. That's up to 3000 words in one hour! I would have smoke coming out of my keyboard and multiple instances of RSI up both my arms in order to achieve that kind of word count normally.

I can't enthuse enough about transcription. By going into the DragonBar menu options, you can change the setting to show the "classic" DragonBar in Windows. If you click the downward arrow on the right hand side of the bar to expand it, you'll see a set of playback controls.

The Classic or Floating DragonBar provides playback controls so you can listen back to your transcribed file and easily find words Dragon recognised incorrectly.

Once you have imported a file for transcription, use these to position your cursor and play that section back. The program will output your audio file (it can be strange hearing your voice in this way, so don't freak out) and this will enable you to correct any areas Dragon has got incorrect if you can't remember exactly what it was you said. Sadly, this option isn't included in the Mac version.

Try to keep your transcription recordings to around a maximum of 20 to 25 minutes. Beyond this, the amount of dictation the program needs to transcribe becomes huge and you'll find your computer is tied up for very long periods of time.

Using Dictation to Make Editing Easier

I strongly do not recommend using Dragon during your editing phase. I'm sure that there will be many authors who want to try this and, if you feel completely comfortable with the software by this stage, go for it. But I don't completely see the point, if I'm honest.

Unless you are someone who needs to use Dragon to control your computer in some way (maybe due to a physical disability), there is simply no need to use Dragon beyond pure dictation. That's something I've found valuable to accept – as a writer, Dragon shouldn't completely remove my need to use a keyboard and mouse. Far from it. Reducing their usage is important, obviously, but there are times when it is simply easier to correct an error using traditional input methods.

This is why I strongly advocate using Dragon simply to complete your first draft. Beyond that, when you enter the editing phase, you can use your keyboard and mouse to make changes to your document. Dragon's job is done at this point – giving you a completed first draft in a much shorter time than if you had typed it.

It's important, then, to highlight some of the ways in which you can use Dragon to get to that completed first draft more quickly and effectively. There is a gigantic amount of commands that the software can accept, but as a writer I think it's vital you stick to just a handful of important ones. These include:

- **scratch that** (to delete the last section of dictation you spoke)

- **copy that** and **paste that**
- **capitalise that** (if you want to capitalise the last thing you said; to do this to something in another part of your document simply say "**capitalise** *words you want to capitalise*")
- **new line** and **new paragraph**
- **select** *words you want selected* (to select an area of text to change but without correcting Dragon – simply speak the new words when the area is highlighted)
- **correct that** or **correct** *words to be corrected* (this will give you a list of choices that Dragon may have misrecognised; choose the correct one or use "spell that" to train the software)

There aren't many commands beyond this that the average writer should need to use. Again, we are not using Dragon for editing so things like bold and italics can be manually added in your word processor later, although if you do want to do this via Dragon you can simply use those commands as well. The problem with using too many commands when you are simply trying to put together a first draft is that sometimes Dragon mixes up something you've tried to dictate with a command; in other words, you could say:

She knew she had broken his heart but that was never her intention.

However, Dragon may output something like this:

She knew she had broken his heart **was never her intention**.

Do you see what's happened here? Dragon has misheard the phrase "but that" and thought that you said "bold that", putting the next part of the sentence in bold! This is a common problem when using DragonPad or Microsoft Word or any other word processor that enables formatting of some kind. Again, this is why I advocate using a plain text editor like Notepad, as Dragon wouldn't be able to apply the bold formatting and would probably figure out you were actually saying "but that" because of the program you are using.

Even worse is when you say something that Dragon misinterprets as a command to select or even cut an area of text you've written. I've had this happen, though it is rare and I managed to catch it just in time. If it happens to you, simply use the command "undo" to restore anything that was accidentally selected or deleted.

If you are finding Dragon is commonly misinterpreting some of your words for commands, you can switch to the "dictation only" mode within the program.

By switching off "Dictation & Commands" you reduce the risk of Dragon making unwanted changes to your text as you dictate.

By default, Dragon listens for both dictation and commands, so change it to this mode if you purely want Dragon to interpret your voice as text. Bear in mind that this will also remove your ability to use commands such as "scratch that" and "correct that". The dictation mode is just that – pure text recognition, nothing else.

What About Punctuation?

The bane of every writer who decides to go down the path of using Dragon is the impending horror of having to dictate punctuation. There is no way around this – you have to get used to it, simple as that. Surprisingly, you quickly get used to dictating your punctuation, especially if you are a writer of non-fiction. There's no doubt about it, non-fiction is much easier to dictate than fiction as, for the most part, you can simply get into a train of thought and speak away. Fiction, on the other hand, requires your characters to interact and – *shock, horror!* – speak to each other.

Dictating dialogue can be a real problem. Consider the following interchange:

"Where did John go? I thought he was meeting you at the station at midday?"

Angela looked worried. "He never arrived. I'm starting to think something terrible may have happened to him."

"Don't panic just yet," James said, placing a hand on her shoulder. "It's too early to jump to any conclusions. Besides, we have work to do."

In order to correctly dictate the above passage into Dragon, this is what you would have to say (I've emphasised the punctuation and used the British *full stop* instead of the American *period*):

Open quote where did John go *question mark* I thought he was meeting you at the station at midday *question mark close quote* Angela looked worried *full stop open quote* he never arrived *full stop* I'm starting to think something terrible may have happened to him *full stop close quote open quote* don't panic just yet *comma close quote* James said *comma* placing a hand on her shoulder *full stop open quote* It's too early to jump to any conclusions *full stop* besides *comma* we have work to do *full stop close quote*

That is the stuff of nightmares, right? When you first start dictating dialogue with Dragon, it can feel incredibly clunky and, to some extent, quite difficult. It takes a fair bit of concentration to get all those commas and quotes in the right places. But, again, remember that what we are creating here is simply a first draft. If you accidentally miss a few out, just keep going. Correct it later in editing.

You may find that after some time getting used to dictation, you start to think in terms of speaking to Dragon. Whenever you write a letter, for example, or an email you will start to speak the punctuation out loud! This isn't uncommon and indicates that you are becoming comfortable with dictation as opposed to typing. The muscle memory of inserting punctuation with your fingers on a keyboard has simply transferred from your fingers to your mouth. The brain process is essentially the same; you are simply diverting the route to get those characters onto the screen.

Mac Users and the Roaming Cursor

It's important at this point to note one of the major problems Mac users encounter when using Dragon – the cursor going walkabout. It's a bug that has plagued Dragon for years and, in the latest Professional for Mac 6, still isn't fixed (and, based on reports from users, may now be even worse). It's hard to pin down exactly why this happens, but it appears to be down to the fundamental differences between the way Dragon interacts between the operating system in the Mac and Windows versions.

It's particularly frustrating when your dictation is flowing and your cursor suddenly decides to have a mind of its own and go on a journey halfway up the page, inserting whatever you continue to dictate in the middle of a previous paragraph. It can also cause havoc when making corrections or inserting punctuation as we've outlined above.

There is an imperfect solution, though. Every now and again (roughly every couple of paragraphs) simply say *"Cache Document"*. This tells Dragon to rescan what you've already dictated, causing it to become less "confused". If things really start to go haywire, say *"Purge Cache"*. This is the nuclear option; it prevents Dragon from being able to make further corrections. It's like hitting the reset button on everything you've dictated so far.

If you still find the cursor is behaving erratically, simply exit Dragon and reopen it. It is inconvenient, to say the least, but it avoids further frustration. One of the most important things you can do as a Mac user, however, is to **make sure you don't touch the keyboard when**

you are dictating. Many people are oblivious to the fact that the Mac software doesn't like you mixing talking and typing. Once you've exited Dragon, you can make changes with the keyboard to your hearts content, but don't do it while the program is running.

These aren't issues that affect PC users or anyone running Dragon for Windows on a Mac in a virtual machine. But if you are using the Mac version of the software, these tips can hopefully make some of its quirks a bit more bearable.

Afterword: Mission Accomplished

I hope this book has been useful to you. Dragon has changed my life for the better in many ways. I no longer worry about getting repetitive strain injuries. My back problems are significantly better as I no longer have to spend hours in a chair, hunched over a desk typing. Aside from the obvious health benefits, I now know I can be more productive than ever before. To be able to churn out up to 3000 words in just one hour, even if those blocks of 15 to 20 minutes are spread throughout the day, is astounding.

One thing that Dragon his taught me is that I am now only limited by my own creativity. We are all the same, whether we are writers, doctors or any other profession. We are all human. We all have just 24 hours in a day. We suffer from the same ailments and time management issues. Using speech recognition helps us to not only avoid some of these health problems but also become more productive in a shorter period of time.

I hope this book has been useful to you and, if you followed some of the tips on how to set up both your hardware and software, you are achieving excellent recognition results. But merely using the software is only the beginning. The beauty of Dragon is that it should get better over time, the more you dictate to it. The issue isn't the software, it's your willingness to use it.

We are all creatives and that can be both an invigorating and challenging profession. The unending horror of a blank page, staring at you mockingly from your screen as you desperately try to find those first words to write, is the bane of any author. Taking that first step and writing those first words is the biggest challenge of all that we face as writers. Just starting is the most important thing and also the most difficult.

You need to retrain your brain, in many ways, to start speaking instead of typing. What if you *had* to do this? What if you had no choice? If your income depended on it, could you bear the thought of being unable to write? When we aren't faced with these difficult choices, we find it easy to make excuses not to do something. It's the classic path of least resistance – not being able to envisage the ability to dictate, telling yourself you can't get used to it, believing your "voice" is somehow different. But this is just all smoke and mirrors. We have always changed the way we write. We transitioned from typewriters to electric typewriters to computers to tablets and even smartphones without an issue. The only constant was that we always used our fingers.

Dragon is simply a different way of achieving

the same result and, in many ways, enables you to unleash your inner storyteller by speaking your words rather than simply typing them. If you can make this mental leap, you are well on your way to not only incorporating dictation successfully into your workflow, but opening up huge potential for the future.

If you embrace Dragon and what it can do, think about the volume of work you can start to achieve. All those words, all those stories could simply fall from your lips far more easily and quickly than you ever could have typed them. To be able to take your creativity and put it out into the world at a much faster rate and, hopefully, reach more readers and sell more books in the process is an incredible thing.

After many years of using Dragon and the speech recognition built into other devices, I now feel shackled by typing. It slows me down and takes up too much of my valuable time. That's time I could have spent marketing my books, a necessary activity for every author these days, or engaging with my readers; time I could have spent with my family, chilling out and relaxing, going for a meal or simply reading a book. That time is precious to me and I'm sure it is to you, too.

I no longer view Dragon as a beast that must be slayed; instead, it has become not only an integral part of my workflow but an incredible tool that has changed both my work and personal life for the better. I'll always be grateful to the incredibly smart people who make this software and keep pushing technology further to enable us to even do these things.

Remember earlier in the book how I said speech recognition software was like a dog riding a bicycle, that it might look ugly but it shouldn't even be possible at all? Well, if that's the case then I'll take it. The pooch might be ugly, but he is truly a writer's best friend. Software like Dragon can actually make us all richer, more productive writers in the long-term.

For that, we should be incredibly grateful.

Additional Resources

It was never my intention to simply release this book and leave you to your own devices to figure things out. There are still many aspects of dictation that can be technically confusing – everything from setup of the software down to which microphones to spend your hard earned money on.

With this in mind, I've put together some **exclusive video content** to help you through this minefield. These are private videos, exclusive to anyone who has bought this book. It's my personal way of saying thank you for your purchase.

To access the free training, go to:
http://eepurl.com/bQ4Y9X

When you enter your email address, you will be sent a private link to the video training. Don't worry – your email address will only be used to send you further videos and details of related releases, including free updates to this book. It will never, ever be shared with or sold to third parties, used for spam or any other purpose.

I have also compiled a list of items featured in this book (and many more not mentioned here) to research and purchase online. These include microphones, software, USB interfaces, apps, voice recorders and much more.

Access the guide at:

https://scottbakerbooks.wordpress.com/ resources/

Now… *Get dictating!*

Made in the USA
Middletown, DE
27 August 2017